Who Do You Think You Are?

*The smart girls guide to creating the life she wants,
with Beauty, Brains and Brilliance.*

…and how I learned to create it all in my life!

Donna Ferrante

BellaDonna Publishing

Who Do You Think You Are?

ISBN-13: 978-0692480878

For more information, please visit:
www.BrillianceFactor.com
or email TheBrillianceFactor@gmail.com

BellaDonna Publishing

For every woman who desires a beautiful

life for herself. Everything you want

is within your reach.

Understand that within these pages,

you may experience what feels like a bit of repetition.

This is intentional.

Repetition creates knowledge. Knowledge creates new habit.

Developing new habits will enable you to pull it all together

and create a life you love.

CONTENTS

ACKNOWLEDGMENTS

This book is dedicated to all of the wonderful women, men, friends, loves, family, coaches, and mentors who have listened, loved, laughed, encouraged, kicked me in the ass, and accompanied me throughout my journey.

…and now it's time to share the knowledge…

FOREWARD

By Cara Alwill Leyba

When I was three years old, my mother enrolled me in dancing school. Let me rephrase that: When I was three years old, I demanded my mother enroll me in dancing school. And I also demanded that I have a pink tutu and a vinyl, square-shaped ballet box with a drawing of a dancer on it (you know, the one all the "big girls" had).

By the third day, I was dancing in the center of the room, bumping the other girls out of the way. I refused to answer to my name, and insisted I was to be called Maria. When my teacher realized that I wasn't schizophrenic, rather just a *tad* bit dramatic, and well, perhaps overly confident, she informed me that there was nobody signed up for ballet by the name of Maria, so unless I answered to Cara, I would have to leave.

I said I'd leave.

It's clear I had a very strong personality at quite a young age. That three year old ballerina is still very much present in me today at 35, however she disappeared for a while throughout most of my life. She disappeared in a sea of limiting beliefs, mean girls, insecurities, bullies, shitty boyfriends, self-doubt, and fear. She eventually made her grand return, but it took work. *A lot of work.*

I know I'm not alone in having lost a part of my confident self somewhere along the way. That precious self-esteem that my mother instilled in me from birth began to take a nose-dive somewhere in my teens. And by my twenties, it had crashed and burned. I fell in love at 21 and quickly became a professional people pleaser, specifically to my boyfriend at the time. I allowed him to take the wheel and drive me straight into a brick wall of insecurity. I spent seven years in that relationship and by the time it was over, putting myself back together became a full-time job. I worked closely with a therapist for quite a few years, learning how to put myself first, which felt more foreign to me than the Japanese alphabet.

When I finally began to rise from the ashes, I became feverishly obsessed with personal development. When I realized I had the power to completely change my attitude, and in turn, change my life, I decided I needed to help other women do the same. My personal experiences led me to become a certified master life coach and I began working with women, many who were walking in my stilettos that I wore just a few short years ago. I was amazed at how many of them had no idea who they were. I was amazed that I had been that girl, too.

As women, we are natural nurturers. We want to be everything to everyone, and make those around us happy. And that is a fabulous way to be, however the problem occurs when the happiness of others becomes more important than our own happiness. Especially when making others happy takes away from our natural essence.

You've probably been there many times: biting your tongue to make someone else comfortable, choosing a career path because your parents wanted you to, settling on a restaurant to make someone else happy, saying yes because you were too afraid to say no, never taking a chance on your passion because it may not fit into the mold others crafted for you - the list goes on. If you can relate to any of that, ladies, then hear me out: ***cut that shit out right now!***

There is nothing in this world more important than your own self-worth. Developing the courage to be exactly who you want to be is life altering.

You have within you, right this very moment, the power to live a life beyond your wildest imagination. To live so boldly, so passionately, and so happily that your world feels like a dream on a daily basis. And this book is going to give you the tools, strategies and the motivation to get there.

If you've ever walked into a room and been afraid of people saying, "Who does she think she is?" it's probably because you've never defined that for yourself in the first place. This book will change your mindset so profoundly that the next time you walk into a room, you'll be able to proudly say, "This is who I am. And I'm fabulous."

With so much love to the author and every woman reading this book,

Cara Alwill Leyba

Author, Master Life Coach,
Creator of The Champagne
Diet

Just a thought…

"The last thing I want you to think is that I'm suggesting we blame our parents for the way we live our lives. I seriously mean that. I don't blame my parents for anything that is happening in my life. Why? Because I am an adult. I am responsible for everything that happens to me, and everything I do. That's right. All of it. Yes, my parents influenced my thinking, but guess what? They aren't doing it any more. I'm a grown ass woman and I get to choose every single thing that I allow into my life. And so do you."

- Donna

The Psychology of Change

Let me ask you this: Why would any of us ever feel the need to make a change to who we are? Why can't we just sit back and be happy with what we do, how we feel, and who we have become? What is this strange feeling we get as adults? That odd feeling that something might be missing. The feeling that there might be something more for us to do. More for us to become. Something bigger. And the craziest question of all: What exactly *is it* that's missing from our lives? We just can't quite put our finger on it can we? Does that mean we are just plain **broken?**

Well let me tell you right now, before the end of the very first page of this book: Absolutely **nothing** is missing. You are **not broken.** You do not need to be **fixed** in any way. You have everything you need right now, right there with you, inside of you, at this very moment to become exactly who and what you want to become.

Whew! That's kind of a relief, isn't it? To know that it's all right there inside of you, waiting to be discovered and nurtured?

You are everything you need. Right there waiting for you to make some loving decisions and give yourself a gentle push in the most beautiful direction! Waiting for you to take some inspired action and make some **on purpose** forward movement. This inspired action will propel you toward recognizing and releasing the powerful, beautiful individual that you **already are,** but have not quite yet unleashed. Until now.

But before we get into that, let's examine the feeling that there is something missing.

We come by this feeling quite honestly, really. We learn from our parents, our mothers, fathers, or whoever it was that raised us, to be good people. Nothing wrong with that, right? Of course not! We are taught to be good little girls and to please absolutely everyone. We must be sure we don't ever inconvenience anyone, no matter what the circumstances. We grow up having learned how to take care of everyone *but* ourselves. We grow up learning to be nurturers. We help others, take care of others, we are there for everyone other than ourselves. Yes, I said that twice. On purpose. And then, if we aren't comfortable with this, then there must be something wrong with us!

Since this dynamic can be all we know, then naturally we keep on doing it. Over and over. And over. And the more we take care of the people around us, the better we seem to feel about ourselves. It's an unfortunate frantic cycle that usually goes something like this:

Hello everyone! Here I am!
Happy, good, people-pleasing girl here!
Who needs me today? You? You?
What? No one needs me today?
Wait. What have I done wrong?
What's wrong with me?
What is missing?
Something is wrong! Something must be wrong with me!
Oh, there you are, friend in need. You need my help.
I've helped you? Whew!
I'm fulfilled and complete!

And the cycle goes on and on, over and over. It is almost comical. And honestly, you absolutely MUST find the humor in it. I want you to recognize this and have a good laugh at how ridiculous this cycle is! Because you are about to break it!!!

There are many things that will keep this cycle going for us. Since all the people in our lives know how we operate, they just seem to line up, don't they? Even the people we love. There *never* seems to be a shortage of people who we believe "need" us, does there? And we are perfectly ok with it, aren't we?

And then…heaven forbid we don't see somebody we can help, fix, or otherwise take care of, we start SEARCHING for someone! It's just what we do! It's all we know! Because we begin doing this at such a young age, and we continue operating this way through most of our adult lives, we can suddenly find ourselves wondering who we really are? *As though something is missing!* Sound like a jump? A stretch? A leap? It's not, and let me explain…

When a young female spends her entire childhood being a good girl, trying to be sure that no one is ever mad at her and that everyone else is doing well and happy, and then she receives consistent positive feedback for it, she will almost invariably continue that dynamic throughout her youth and well into her teenage years. She may find herself being the teacher's pet. You know the one. She cleans the chalkboard and the erasers. She is the one who sits at the front of her class. It may even look like she has loads of friends! Who *wouldn't* want a friend like that? But in most cases, she doesn't have loads of friends. She just has loads of people who know her. People whom she can "help."

When we examine this more carefully and begin to pay attention to how we are thinking, we begin to recognize the issue. Of course, there is nothing wrong with being the good girl. Every parent in the world wants their little girl to be good, quiet, respectful, sweet, loving. But when these wonderful, sweet qualities become a way of life for a young teenage girl, watch out. This girl can be set up for some tough times in her future.

Of course Mom and Dad are completely unaware of it. All they see is a great girl! It's not their fault either. They are doing the best they can with the knowledge and tools they have at their disposal.

However, at one point or another in her adult life, someone is going to ask our girl what she does, what she likes, what she hates, what she cares the most for. If she's like most women in her situation, she will have a very difficult time answering these types of questions.

You see, when we spend our lives taking care of everyone and excluding ourselves, we never have the opportunity to learn what we like or what we love or even what we dislike. We spend our lives wrapping ourselves around all of the people we spend time with. Especially when it comes to our adult relationships. Does the boy like race cars? Then we like race cars. Does the boy like skiing? Then we like skiing. Does the boy like camping? Then we like camping. Does the boy like Italian food? Then we like Italian food.

It's a dangerous game, not because camping or race cars are bad things, but because when we live this way, we handicap ourselves by never taking the necessary time to discover and nurture who we really are and what we truly love and care about.

Now, if you're a parent reading this, don't hate me. And don't be hard on yourself. Of course none of us would do this intentionally to a young girl. It happens gradually, with out notice or symptom. So as people who are raising and/or influencing these young girls, we definitely need to be aware of the possibility that this is happening. But how do we do that, considering that there are no symptoms to watch for?

Well, that answer my friend, is the "C" word. COMMUNICATION. And of course, LOVE.

One of the most important things we must provide for the young people in our lives, male or female, is a good sense of self, and a high level of self-esteem. But I am not telling you anything you don't already know, right? With the intention of raising a good, respectful, polite, young person, comes the responsibility of making sure their self-esteem is in tact. That takes consistent communication with our young people, making sure they know there is a non-judgmental dialogue open for them. They must know that they can come to us, the adults, when they feel uncomfortable or vulnerable.

Unfortunately for those of us who are living this "serving everyone else" lifestyle, we don't discover that we are neglecting ourselves while we're young and in the middle of it. We just keep forging ahead, doing what we do. Waiting and longing for that few minutes of beautiful gratification that we desperately need to feel. That temporary sense of happiness that we feel when we know we have done something big for someone else. It's fleeting, that gratification, and it's why we continue the hunt for that all important approval from the various people in our lives. It can feel like an addiction, and naturally, we would not wish that upon anyone.

And so it continues for our girl. When she is not feeling that warm and fuzzy feeling she needs so badly, she had better go find someone else to nurture or otherwise fix, because she's sure that big feeling of completion and approval will be there next time. Or the next time. Or the next time. It can be exhausting!

The good news is, it works itself out in the end for most people. However, usually we have to wait until we are adults and some major cataclysmic event happens. Some kind of BIG THING in our lives will wake us up and make us realize that we haven't been taking care of ourselves properly.

For some, it's a relationship change that makes us take notice. For others, it's a job change. Suddenly laid off ? Company downsizing? Passed over for a promotion? (I've been there) Sudden illness? Something HUGE will stop us in our tracks and show us that we've done a horrible job of setting our priorities and boundaries. And because of our lack of self-care and self-love and self-worth, we just might find that when *we* need someone to nurture *us* for a change, the list of people we can call upon is a pretty short one - a pretty much non-existent one.

We've allowed ourselves to be the "strong" ones for so long, and we are just so damn good at it, that the last thing anyone would think is that we might actually need something for ourselves. Damn it! You've been so nice and so accommodating!!! Where the hell did everybody go?

My hope is that realizing all of this will make you stop right in your tracks, and take a good hard look at how you have been living your life.

Let's look at another scenario. Let's say you are one of those lucky individuals who just wakes up one day and says,

"What happened?? I just realized that I have no idea who I am. What do I like? Who am I? What do I want to do? I have no idea, because I've been so focused on helping and fixing everyone else that I never had the time to learn about ME! I have been told how I should act and what I should like all my life! First my parents, and then my unfortunate relationship choices! Shit!!! Now what??? Shit!!! Shit!!!"

And still there are others who wake up quietly one uneventful day and say, *"This just isn't enough."* No drama, no carrying on, just a quiet realization and an awakening, maybe a few tears, and then the big question comes: *"Now what the hell do I do?"*

Whoa! Whoa! Whoa! Stop! Wait! Hang on a minute. Hold the phone. Enough of this heavy, depressing shit!

Let me give you a little reassurance right here, right now. Just knowing that most women will have this realization at some point in their lives should comfort you just a bit. Believe me, you are not alone. And here's some more good news for you: No matter what your situation, or what your age, it is never too late to change things up!

Although yes, it can be extremely frightening to wake up one day and realize that you don't have any hobbies, you don't love your job, you don't know what your favorite color is, or your favorite food, music, or movie, you are in good company. Remember that every woman in this situation has woken up to this realization in one way or another during her life. Or she will soon. And so will you.

Here's the best news yet: Whether you are 20 years old or 70 years old, you have all the time you need to pull it all together. Gracefully. Gently. And with *beauty* and *brains* and *brilliance*. Good news, don't you think? I feel a bit relieved just writing these words!

Let's talk about self-esteem for a moment. Just for the sake of our education, let's examine what good, healthy self-esteem is:

Emily Roberts, MA, LPC says this. "A person who has healthy self-esteem will do things that they know will make them feel good, and often allow themselves to be put first and not feel guilty about it. Healthy self-esteem takes practice. Getting to know who you are, your moods, your likes and dislikes, and your preferences is an ongoing necessity. Self-reflection and a little humor can take you to a place where healthy self-esteem is possible."

This is such GREAT news! So even if we have spent our entire lives taking care of everyone and excluding ourselves from the equation, the healthy self-esteem that has eluded us for a large portion of our lives can be ours! I believe that calls for a celebration!

Pop! Fizz! Clink!

If we expect to learn who we are, what we like, and what we need, we are going to need to spend some quality time with ourselves. Now THAT can be a scary idea. I would like to show you first hand that you are not alone in this struggle by sharing a part of my story with you:

At the point in my life when I learned that I had lived this life of taking care of everyone but myself, I made the decision to speak with a therapist for a year or so. I had just gone through a painful divorce and I thought I was *brilliant* for coming up with this plan to help myself! I was so proud of myself for choosing to look for help in understanding what happened - to be sure it wouldn't happen again. Well, as it turned out, the brilliant one was *not* me. It was my Therapist. She asked me to tell her exactly how I wanted to move on. She asked me what I liked, loved, wanted to do, etc. Well guess what? I had absolutely no *freaking* idea.

What she taught me turned it all around for me like a lightening bolt. I am going to suggest that you learn this the same way I did. It is a beautiful and wonderful practice and even if you believe you have it all together in every way, I know this would be a good process for you to go through once or twice or three times. Or four.

Here is how it works. I will tell you honestly, make sure when you do this when you have some time alone. It will not be effective if you get interrupted. I don't want you to put this off, but at the same time, I want you to give yourself at least 30 uninterrupted minutes alone to go through it.

Ready? Here we go:

Imagine yourself as an 8 year old little girl. Take the time to get that picture in your mind. Remember clearly what you looked like as an 8 year old. Now imagine that you are sitting beside your 8 year old self.

Look carefully at her and see the details. Notice what she looks like. Is she cute? Of course she is! What is she wearing? Is she carrying anything? A little girl purse, a stuffed animal, a book? What do her shoes look like? Is she wearing a dress, a skirt and blouse? Little girl shorts? What does her hair look like? Is there a bow in her hair or a pony tail? Take your time with the details and get a clear picture of her in your mind.

Now, just sit with her for a little while and be in her presence. Spend some quiet time with her, thinking about her, looking at her. Pretend that she is real and sitting with you. Once you have a clear picture of her in your mind, make a point of remembering that picture. Keep her with you and think of her as your new little friend. Sounds strange, I know. Stay with me here.

Now, in your mind or out loud, whatever works for you, ask her what she would like to do today. You are going to begin to take care of this little girl right now! Tell her you're going to take her out for a day, anywhere she wants to go, and anything she wants to do! Ask her how she wants to spend the day. Pay attention to how she is answering you. Is she shy? Where does she want you to take her? What does she want to do? Go to a park? Get ice cream? Go to a movie? I bet she can answer you pretty quickly, right? Interesting...

Here is what you need to do next. Go out "with" her. Spend an afternoon out, alone with her. Just the two of you. Let her hold your hand. Do absolutely anything she wants to do. Take your 8 year old self out for a fun afternoon and get to know her. Notice what she likes, what she doesn't like. What makes her happy? What makes her giddy with laughter? What makes her feel tickled inside?

The more time you spend getting to know HER, the more time you spend getting to know YOU. If you do this once or twice, you will start to learn what you really like. And you may be very surprised at what that is.

*****

Many women easily abandon their childhood and never look back, never taking the time to think about themselves as children, now that they are "grown up." But if you do the things you loved when you were a child, you will get much closer to your passion and your brilliance as an adult. You will be able to learn what lights you up, maybe for the very first time in your life.

I know this may sound foreign to you and maybe even extremely odd, but believe me, you will get a lot out of this exercise. If you were raised like I was, where absolutely everyone else in the world must come first, then it's about damn time you got to know yourself a little better. Don't you agree?

Final note: Do not speak out loud to your 8 year old self if you are on the subway. People will think you're crazy and run from you.

After you've completed this exercise, make some notes for yourself. How did this feel? Have you learned anything? Do you feel as though this is something you should go through again?

_____

_____

_____

_____

_____

_____

_____

_____

_____

_____

_____

_____

_____

_____

_____

_____

_____

_____

_____

_____

The Most Brilliant Question
You Will Ever Ask:

I have never been the type of person to make anyone wait. Probably because I hate waiting for anything myself. So I'm just going to tell you the most brilliant question you'll ever ask yourself, before I even start discussing it:

"WHO DO I WANT TO BECOME?"

Go ahead. Ask yourself. Say it out loud. Do it! Just sit with it for a minute. Asking and answering this question will not be as easy as it seems! Many people would rather run from it, but not you, right? You are a brilliant person - of course you are, you want to better yourself! You are leagues ahead of others who for some reason just blindly accept things as they are!

There are a great number of people who think and live their lives with this philosophy:

"I am what I am, I am who I am, and that's enough. Everyone will just have to accept me the way I am."

If this is you my love, then CHEERS to you! Pop! Fizz! Clink! Congratulations on all of the self-reflection, study and hard work you have done to get yourself to exactly where you truly want and need to be!! *(gentle sarcasm intended!)*

I feel very strongly about this. Right now, not someday, do yourself a favor and ask this question:

Who Do I Want to Become?

Ask it over and over. Ask it a lot. Ask it every day. Ask it separately in regards to the various areas of your life, one at a time. Ask it and write notes in the margins of this book! Are you beginning to understand how seriously I am taking this question?

Asking and answering this question will push you into the direction you want to go. Into the place where you will find your most brilliant life. We are going to get into this more deeply, and it will change many things for you. That is a promise!

This is seriously a life changing question once you learn what to do with it and how to work it! And I am just the girl to show you how to do it! I'm excited to start this process with you! Get ready for a bit of a ride babe, because you are certainly in for one. It is especially exciting, because now you get to bring your 8 year old self, your new little best friend along for the ride!

To be clear, you are going to want to ask this question any time you are considering making a change in your life. This question is going to be another new best friend. "Who do I Want to Become?"

Let's examine some of the different areas that exist in any given life. These are the types of categories that people struggle with. These are the areas that separate us from one another. Even though there are things that are important to you, which may not be important to me, you will see that there are some common threads among us.

These common areas are the places where people often set goals for themselves. Sometimes they set lofty, scary goals with no idea of how they will meet them! That's a very good thing! A mentor of mine, ages ago, told me that if I didn't have an upset stomach, my goals were not set high enough. Well, my love, I'm going to try very hard NOT to upset your stomach. You can write to me and let me know how it goes!

Here are some of the areas where people feel the need to make changes in their lives. Read through them and see if there is some-thing there that strikes a chord with you. Ready? Let's do this!

Your Education. This was a really big one for me. I was the second person in my entire family, including the extended family, to get any sort of university education. This was something that set me far apart from my immediate family. And not in a good way.   In fact, talk about push back! I had my Master's Degree before my Mother even knew I'd started studying at all. It was something that was so foreign to my family that there was no connection at all around the subject. If the subject of education was brought up, it was changed within a few minutes. More later on this!

Your Home Surroundings. How did you grow up? Was your house clean? Was your Mother a neat freak? Was she a germaphobe? Was she a busy woman with several children who she had to take care of in addition to working to support you and your siblings? Was she June Cleaver? Did she greet your father at the door each day with a Martini?

Your Accent. Whoa! Wait a minute! Can this be changed? Well, of course it can! I did it, and many others have done it. But really! Talk about a "Who do you think you are?" moment! You don't want the accent that everyone you know has and that you grew up with? Why not? Why do you think you're better than the people you grew up with? Just kidding. I'm not asking you that. What I am telling you is that *someone else will.* There is nothing wrong with wanting to change that twang! Your accent can dictate how you are perceived by others. I get it. That's why I consciously made the effort to remove my Pittsburgh accent from my life! I LOVE Pittsburgh. I just didn't love the accent. So I can completely relate if you feel that way. Sound trivial? It's not. Let's move on...

Your Religion. Wow. Hold on tight with this one. I did this, too. Talk about creating a canyon between you and your parents! But people do it all the time. For most people, it just turns into the elephant in the room. The big subject that everyone is thinking about but no one will discuss. Trust me when I say, it is better to under- stand the fear and concern that your family has for your newly "un-saved" soul than to keep your head buried in the sand. If you have religious controversy, I would suggest you deal with it sooner rather than later.

Your Sense of Style. This is actually my favorite one! Our style can change many times during our lives as we enter various seasons of learning about who we are. If you're a new mom, you may find your style changing simply because you don't have time now to worry about it! If you've started a new or more professional job, you will definitely need to visit your style choices! Or maybe like me, you grew up in Blue Jean-ville! Where no one dressed up for anything. Ever. Maybe church. But remember, I gave that up! So what happens now, when after choosing a distinctly European style of dress for myself, I go home to visit my family? You got it. Push back. Big time. It's actually very funny to me now. I seem to have rubbed off onto some of my relatives. Frump to Fab! And that works just fine for me!

Your Makeup. I could have included this one with STYLE, but I love makeup so much, I wanted to address it separately. Did you grow up in a religion where makeup was forbidden? I did. Did you grow up in New England where Birkenstocks are worn to church? Where Crocs are worn to weddings? Where the women, bless their hearts, let their gray hair grow out, long and wiry? Where Chapstick is considered "Dolled up?" I know that sounds gross, but I have experienced it. Not ME! God, no! But I had friends when I lived in Connecticut who wore their hair like this and couldn't have cared less how they looked. And in my experience, it was not a wonderful self-confidence level that allowed them to choose to appear this way. It was obstinance. It was an over-compensation of insecurity. It was, "Damn it, no one will tell me what to do." With maybe just a little laziness thrown in. Sorry ladies, but you know I'm right about this.

Now of course, everyone in Connecticut isn't this way. Remember *I* lived there. And there were a few others besides myself who dressed up and wore makeup every day. But I was certainly exposed to many women who were completely comfortable rolling out of bed, not washing their faces, not brushing their hair and insisting that everyone accept them just the way they were. Ugh!

The Way You Speak. Accent excluded. Seriously, have you HEARD a Pittsburgh accent? But I already covered that. This is about more than that. This is about using proper grammar. Proper volume. Proper pronunciation. Proper enunciation. I believe it is more about having a good command of the English language and not sounding like you just came home from 6 years at your Uncle Buck's dude ranch. NOT that there's anything wrong with your Uncle Buck's dude ranch! But if you are meeting with a prospective client or employer, you may want to punch it up just a bit. Then, hang on to your cowboy hat, y'all. Your family is going to act as though they don't recognize you. How about your friends, who now want to know why you think you're better than they are?? Drama, baby, drama!

Your Heart's Desires. This is a big one. Here are some examples of this. If you've come from a family where no one ever goes anywhere and now your heart's desire is to travel. Or if you've come from a meat and potatoes eating family and now you're a vegetarian. Or if you've come from a Country Music household and you love Classical Music (me). What if you've come from a family of people who don't really enjoy participating in activities such as sports in high school, or school plays, musicals, science fairs, etc., and now you're expecting your family to come to see you at the local Theatre group you joined?

At one point, I was so happy because I had FINALLY gotten my parents to come see me sing with a Symphony Orchestra Choir in Johnstown, Pennsylvania. It took a LOT of convincing to get them to come, but I did it. And then, *Voila!* My Dad fell asleep right in the middle of the orchestra performing the William Tell Overture. Now do not get me wrong, I have a great relationship with my Dad. He never knew this, but I was completely heart broken when that happened. When the show was over and I went to meet my parents to ask them what they thought, all they said to me was, "We better head back home." I must have cried for a week once they left town. Their fault? Nope. Mine!

OH! YOUR HAIR, MY GOD! MY GOD, YOUR HAIR! Here
is a self-esteem crusher, if there ever was one! Every time I'd go to visit my parents, it seemed like I had a different hair style. Which goes back to having no clue who I was or what I liked! I think my mom was heartbroken when I announced that I hated Perms and she should hate them too! But it needed to be said, damn it! No 20 year old girl should have hair like her Grandmother. Cut short, permed and round. Really??? It's how I grew up. I feel very strongly about this one! So when I grew out my super-cute, sleek, Chanel style bob, and went to see my mother, I was met with: "Oh, you're wearing your hair like that." Seriously??? Yes I damn well am! I just cried by myself when I went to bed that night. She never knew. Her fault? Nope. Mine.

Your Weight. This is a difficult subject because so many women struggle with their weight at different times during their lives. I was no exception. A season of fat, a season of thin, a season of fat, a season of thin. Can you relate to this? My Mother came to visit me in Connecticut one time and wanted to take a picture of me home with her, which I thought was so sweet! When I gave her one, she smiled and said, "I can't wait to get back and tell everyone how matronly you have become." To quote Bridget Jones, "F*******************CK!" Matronly? Me? This was one of my THIN photos. Matronly? She should have just slapped me. It would have hurt much less. She's going to **SHOW EVERYONE** that I'm *Matronly* now. Ahh, motherly love in action!

Are you finding some of the humor in this? I sure hope so. Let's move on.

What You Read. Everything you read needs to support who you are and who you choose to be. I personally am not a night time reader. I bring a book with me almost everywhere I go. I want to read when I'm alert and awake and can really focus on what it is I'm pouring myself into. Did you come from a family of readers? I will tell you about my friend Connie. She comes from a family of TV watchers. Not that there's anything wrong with that, but if you come a family who thinks that reading an actual book is **WOOWOO,** expect some push back! And if you come from a family who will only read the latest Jackie Collins book, or some kind of Comedy book, also, expect some push back.

What You Drink. Do you love wine? I love Champagne. If you've come from a family who believes that alcohol is evil, you can expect some serious push back. Especially where religion is involved. This is a subject that can create the most argumentative environment. Fortunately for me, we like our alcohol in my family. My people are Italian. I've been drinking mediocre to bad red wine since I was 14. By the time I was 30 or so, I'd visited Napa Valley 3 or 4 times and had gotten quite the education from the wine growers of California. I remember the first time I'd brought home a good bottle of wine. It was Chardonnay from the Chateau Montelena Winery. If you are ever blessed with the opportunity to visit this Winery, please do.

The Montelena people are wonderful and they have one of the most beautiful wineries in California. So back to my story. Of course, my Reunite drinking family HATED the $80 bottle that I'd purchased. Good for me, right? Over two days, I got to drink it all myself. They made every silly looking, icky yuk face you can imagine. You'd have thought I'd given them gasoline to drink. I may as well have. I never really had to call myself a wine snob. My parents did that for me. Along with telling me how wrong and crazy I was. Push back!

So there you are. Just a few places in our lives where we need to visit, spend time in, and make choices around. I have addressed these specific areas individually because I have experienced them. But under- stand, everyone of us has had a different experience with our families and our upbringing. There may be 10 other areas where you would like to better yourself and can expect push back.

*****

For now, let's talk a bit in more general terms. Let's talk about those "mean" parents of ours!

You need to know right now, that I am one hundred percent against blaming our parents for our pasts and for holding how we were raised against them. That is not what this book is about. This is about YOU, my love. It's about how YOU are going to manage your life and how YOU are going to turn it into the most Brilliantly Passionate Lifestyle you have ever experienced. Despite how you were raised!

First of all, God bless all of our parents. They did the best they could do with the tools they had at their disposal. Remember the times! When were you being raised? What was going on in our country then? And just as important is this: How and when were your parents raised? During the Great Depression? During the 50's, 60's, 70's, 80's? Each decade has had is own set of challenges and struggles for people who were raising children. It was never easy.

At one time, only Dad worked. Mom always stayed home to cook and clean. So when a child was added into the mix, most of the time she had to add caring for that child into her life with no additional help. Dad was busy earning a living. He came home as tired as his wife, the new Mom. Keep this in mind and give them a break! You are an adult now. There is no need to blame anyone! And remember - keep looking for the humor!

Let's visit another scenario. Were you raised by a single parent? A Mom alone or a Dad alone? Shit! Talk about PRESSURE! I see many of my friends and acquaintances raising children as single parents, and even now in 2015, it's *really* hard. I honestly just cannot imagine how they do it! I am continually amazed at how little support is available for single parents. If they work at all, and they almost always do, even the smallest wage is too much income for them to qualify for any help! This seriously pisses me off!

When those children grow up, they are going to be looking at their lives and asking themselves who they want to become! It is totally understandable that there will be things that they don't want to repeat with their own children. Let's hope they don't blame their parents for who they've become!

Do you personally know any single parents? I bet you do. Ask them how easy it's been for them. Ask them how many nights of sleep they've lost or how hard it has been to find a baby sitter, or how incredibly difficult and expensive it is to put their child in day care so they can go to work and try to make a living. I think you'll find that it's much harder on them than you've ever imagined. You might even find yourself wanting to help them out once you hear their stories. In fact, I'd be surprised if you didn't try to find a way to help them - and you should! Especially if your biggest complaint is that your Mom never liked your hair or your makeup!

Rant over. Sorry about that. I just had to put it all out there. Blame my parents. Just kidding!

In our next Chapter, we're going to examine 12 areas that I will ask you to think about for yourself. Each of these are areas in my life where I've chosen to make changes in order to push myself toward who I would like to become.

Please understand that this is a process. It will take you longer to determine the areas in your life where you'd like to make positive changes, than it will to read this book. And it will take you even more time than that to get through the process of changing. I suggest that you get yourself ready for a long, enlightening, wonderful journey!

I think we should celebrate again!!! Pop! Fizz! Clink! Cheers!

You are going to find that some areas in your life are more easily modified than others. Some, if you're like me, will be a life long journey. And like me, you need to be ok with that. I am making light of some of the points that I'm sharing with you, but you need to under- stand that this is a very important subject. This is YOUR LIFE, and YOUR HAPPINESS we're creating here. Everything has to be done your way and within a time frame that suits your personal desires.

SO. NOW. ASK THE BIG QUESTION.

WHO DO YOU WANT TO BECOME?

Do not underestimate even for a second, the importance of what you are doing here. These changes are going to give you what I keep writing about: *The most brilliantly passionate lifestyle you've ever lived.* Are you excited? I hope you are. Once we start dealing with the push back you are going to receive - and you are going to receive some push back - things are going to get very exciting for you!!!

Awareness and Mindset Shift

By now, I'm sure you're starting to understand where I'm going with this philosophy. You examine your life, acknowledge where you've come from and where you've been, make a conscious, on purpose decision about who you want to become, and start living that life right now. Easy, right? Hell no! But let's keep going.

If you can learn to compartmentalize your thoughts and your needs and desires and begin to think about each area of your life separately, you will find that you can get clear quite quickly on what you truly want and love and need in your life.

There are exercises that I go through with my Coaching Clients that bring them to these answers lightning fast. Reading about it may take a bit longer, but I promise you it will be well worth it. What I'm teaching you and what you are learning is the art of becoming aware of and making changes to your mindset.

When you give thought to this subject and start to make some on purpose decisions, you are going to feel a huge shift in your life. If you're like me, you will also feel a great weight lifted off of your shoulders. There is peace in knowing who you really are. There is joy in figuring out what changes you need to make in order to get there, and even more joy and love in living the life you have taken the time to create for yourself.

There are so many women out there who tell me they have absolutely no idea what they want their lives to look like. You are not that woman. You are becoming aware that you have a choice as to what you accept into, and eliminate from your life. I think once we touch on the concept of mindset and how you view what you want in your life, you'll find more areas in your life that you can add to the mix of the new and improved YOU.

In the last Chapter, I discussed 12 areas where I personally chose to better myself. I'm going to review those areas again, but this time I'm going to give you some examples of what it means to shift your mindset and begin thinking about some changes that you may choose to implement into your life. Your mindset is everything. Now that you are learning that you are in control of how you feel about, think of and react to any given situation, you understand that you get to CHOOSE your mindset.

Let's just dive into it, shall we?

I am going to offer you a mindset shift to consider for each of the categories I've discussed. Some of the mindset shifts you will see pop up in more than one category and I will explain how they apply to you as we move through the information.

*****

Education. Whether or not this is a good time in your life to go back to school doesn't matter. Of course, if you can do that and you really desire it, I am all for it. I firmly believe that there is no such thing as too much knowledge and education.

College or not, we continually educate ourselves for our entire lives. Whether we're reading Vogue Magazine, or Poems from Rumi, we're still learning. As a self-aware woman who wants to choose who she will become, rather than evolving mindlessly, you are going to want to choose what you surround yourself with.

In this area of our lives, we're talking about books. So ask yourself this: What books have you accumulated on your bookshelves? What magazines to you read? I admit, I will read through a tabloid or two while I'm in the grocery store line, but I am much more careful when I'm deciding what to purchase and what I want to bring into my home. I choose to surround myself with books and magazines that represent who I have chosen to become.

Gone are the books that do not serve me in my quest for becoming my best self! Gone are the Diet Books, the Shape Books - Oh, how depressing those are! I surround myself with the most beautiful books about Paris - because I am a serious Francophile! Books about Fashion Designers and Musicians! Books about writing and books with pictures of beautiful clothing in them. This is what I love. This is what I want surrounding me at all times. I want to have lots of what I LOVE, not things that will depress me by pushing me into a direction that doesn't make me happy.

Mindset Shift: **Curate** rather than **Accumulate.**

If you carefully choose the reading materials that you surround yourself with, you will nourish your mind and soul with only the most beautiful, only the chosen materials that bring you the brilliant and passionate lifestyle you are craving. Educate yourself with the best information that you can find on any subject that you love. Give yourself that gift. What do you love? Poetry, Decorating, Animals, Plants, or Cooking? There is no wrong answer. Just make sure you are surrounding yourself with what you love. This will enable you to **Curate** your life as opposed to **Accumulating** things randomly.

Here's an important thought. Before you start running out buying up books and magazines, take some time to de-clutter your space and your former mindset. Do yourself a favor and get rid of every book or magazine you own that has not contributed to the life you want to live. If it doesn't make you feel special, smart, talented, and tickled inside, say bye-bye.   Let's move on:

Home Surroundings. This is a super important area for you to consider when designing your life. We all know that our homes tell the story of who we are. So I ask you this: Does your home tell your story? Ask yourself, am I really who my home says I am? Am I really this messy? (if your home is messy)   You must be sure that your home represents the IDEAL YOU. So as you can see once again, we're asking that all important question: Who do you want to become?

You must do everything that you can do to make your home your sanctuary. Your nest. Your place of peace. Recreate your home so that it represents exactly who you want to become. Doing this will enable you to be that better version of yourself right away. No waiting for this or that to happen. No waiting until you have a million dollars in the bank, or you are in the perfect relationship. No waiting until you have the perfect home. Even if you live in a tiny apartment, make it the best it can be RIGHT NOW.

Mindset Shift: **Beautify** rather than **Clutter**.

This can mean taking the necessary time to declutter your home. I always suggest decluttering one area of your home at a time to keep it manageable. It can mean throwing away or donating a lot of items that may have served you at one time, but do so no longer. Find a good charity and let your things help someone else to become their best self. We all know that one woman's gym suit is another woman's tutu. Let someone else shine when they find the pieces you've let go of.

I truly think decluttering is a freeing exercise that will open you up to receiving more of what you really want in your life. Remember that everything is energy. By getting rid of your negative or neutral energy items, and only allowing items that help you create your new life, you'll continue to attract more positive energy into your world. So when you are working on your home, embrace the mindset of **Beautification.** It is so much more *new you* than **Clutter!**

Ready for more? Of course you are!

Your Accent. This is actually a fun subject for me because as I mentioned, I personally have had an accent that I wanted to stop hearing come out of my mouth. Now don't get me wrong, my Pittsburgh friends. A Pittsburgh accent can be a beautiful thing. Just not for me. It just isn't the way I want to see myself, now that I'm work- ing on purpose to create my life. There are online courses you can take that you will find by Googling them if you'd like. I just chose to sing! Have you ever noticed that when a vocalist is singing you can't hear an accent? Hmmm. Interesting. Once I realized that, I started singing, and really listening to how I sounded. I still don't like the sound of my own speaking voice. I don't think anyone likes their own voice! But I recorded myself speaking anyway, and I made a point of slowing down my speech. I asked friends to stop me if I started talking too fast.

I would listen to a recording of someone's voice that I loved and repeat what they say immediately after they would say is. For me, that was great practice, especially on the slowing down part. The singing helped just because the more you sing, the more comfortable it becomes to pronounce words in a specific way - without the accent.

This has been a struggle and a journey of it's own for me, but I am committed to it. I am also aware that it is going to be something I will work on for the rest of my life. I've accepted that and I will move on. I will not beat myself up because I don't have a smooth, sexy, calming voice. I will just take it one day at a time and do the best I can do to sound the way I would like to sound, because remember, just like you, what I choose is all up to me.

Mindset Shift: **Practice slowly** rather than **Rushing through**.

If in our minds, we think of communicating in terms of gently sharing our thoughts and opinions, it becomes a bit easier to slow down and not bark our ideas at people. And BONUS, you'll find that when you slow down, people are much more likely to get into a good, interesting, stimulating conversation with you. When you're paying attention to how you sound, it makes you easier to be around. People like that. So **practicing** the way you sound will always work better for you than **rushing through your thoughts**!

Moving on…

Your Religion. Ooh baby, this can be a hard one. But it doesn't have to be. Let me explain! Most of us have been raised with a specific set of religious beliefs. Our parents wanted to raise us with a sense of morality and goodness, and who can blame them? As adults, we are able to examine what we've been taught and make our own decisions regarding religion. I did that. I grew up in a very oppressive religion, where anyone who questioned what we were learn- ing was shunned, or thrown out of their house, depending upon their age.

My friend, also part of our church, was a seriously wimpy teenager and always gave in to her parents demands. Her brother was not so quiet about his thoughts. He was also the epitome of stubbornness. He didn't want to change religions, per se, but he did question how his parents treated him. Whether or not he was treated differently than his siblings, I don't know, but that was his perception.

To this day, it breaks my heart to think of this, but I'm going to share it with you. I remember one of the very cold - many degrees below zero - winters that we had in Pittsburgh. This boy's parents told him that he had to leave their house. He was just about 16 years old when that happened, so luckily, he did have a car. He left the house in the snow and ice at night, and went to his girlfriend's house, which was about an hour away from where he lived. She and her family were part of this religion as well.

I found out much later that his girlfriend's parents, those wonderfully religious people told him they didn't have room for him in their house and made him sleep in his car. I was told three nights had passed before he called his mother and asked if he could go back home. The story is, she was very smug and happy, sitting on her high horse, talking about how he gave in and called begging to come home.

Honestly, I am crying right now as I write this. Who makes a 16 year old boy sleep in his car in the middle of the winter in Pittsburgh? Regardless of how much room you have or do not have in your house, you just don't do it. Give the kid a blanket and a place on the floor rather than outside. Damn them.

You see? I'm not perfect. This is a journey for me as well as it is for you. I am seriously pissed off that this happened to this boy. Or ANY child. I dare anyone to tell me that this was an act of kindness offered to a young person from a religious household.

Well. As I always say, Karma is a bigger bitch than I will ever have to be. I hear that this boy is now married with 4 children and will never have a cold winter night in his car again. As for the other family? I could not care less. Karma is my friend.

Mindset Shift: **Consciously Consider** rather than **Blindly accept**.

On the subject of religion, don't just accept what you are told. Question everything! The story I just shared is typical of stories that many of us have when it comes to our religions. Oppression, denial, neglect, arrogance. Of course not all religions or religious people are like this. Just the ones I've been exposed to.

I know first hand, that when you grow up with this type of religious dysfunction, you tend want to think long and hard about how you were raised and how you want religion to be a part of your life as an adult, if at all. So taking the time to **consciously consider** what you are being taught and not just **blindly accepting** what you have been told will increase your education in this area and draw you closer to the type of person you have chosen to become.

Next on our growth list -

Your Signature Style. Whew! Are you ready to lighten things up a bit? I know the religion category was tough to get through. But your style is something different. This my love, is all about fun and glamour! It's about discovering who you are and supporting your choices through your appearance, your clothing, your accessories, and how you choose to present yourself, or show up every day.

As you take the time to examine exactly how you want your life to look in this area, you'll find that your sense of style is a super fun way to create a Brilliant you! Do you want to show up as elegant? Or do you want to show up as edgy? Classic? Preppy? Are you Gaga? Or are you more Audrey? Are you Marilyn? Monroe or Manson? Or are you more Madonna?

When you look through magazines and see the various styles, what are you drawn toward? When you imagine yourself wearing different types of outfits, when do you feel your best? When do you feel like you are unstoppable. I mean: *UNSTOPPABLE!!!* When do you feel like you can take on the world and WIN!? Remember that this is the feeling we are going for here.

When I was determining my style, I made a Pinterest Board and as I was going through looks, I'd add anything that I found exciting onto my board. I highly suggest doing this. After a few weeks of pinning, my style became very clear. When I looked at all of my pins, I saw mostly black. Why? I know feminine girly girls like color! I had to give it a great deal of thought and figure out why I was feeling so good about the non-color that I was continually drawn toward. I am very feminine and very girly, but black Couture called my name!

The reason turned out to be my love of travel. I love Italian women and how they dress. I also love French women and how they dress. As it turns out, I especially love a minimalist approach to choosing clothes. Let me tell you, that was a big lightbulb that went on over my head!

I feel good in black. I feel elegant and sophisticated in black. I feel worldly in black. And I can keep a minimal wardrobe - just like Europeans do - and accessorize to my heart's content. Every day now, I go to my closet and choose my black pants, or skirt du jour, then a top, then if appropriate, a jacket. The color I add is beautiful, but it is all in my accessories. My scarves, my handbags, my shoes, my gloves in the Winter. And that's me! I'm known for it now. I get complements on my outfits daily. If they only knew, I own 4 pairs of black pants and 4 black skirts! The rest of my signature style is all in the accessories! Doesn't that sound fun? Freeing? And talk about an organized closet! I LOVE it!

Mindset Shift: **Curate** rather than **Accumulate**. *(you'll find this is my favorite Mindset Shift!)*

I definitely think this will be the most fun you will have while making changes in your life. Once you choose your style, you'll begin to **curate** your wardrobe like a master stylist and stop **accumulating** all of those random pieces just because they were on sale!

More more more…

Your Makeup. This is another favorite area of mine, as you know!!! I was a makeup artist for Chanel for ages and ages, so I know my sh*t in this area. I was never the type of artist who would sell excessive amounts of products to people. Only what they needed, and only what would make them feel *FABULOUS*. I was the one who would actually talk people *out* of buying things now and then! So I hope you'll trust me on this topic.

First of all, please do yourself this favor: Do not underestimate the power of makeup. Too much is just as bad as too little.

If you're not really a "make up person," then give this some thought:

Let's say you are going to meet someone who is important to you, such as a prospective employer or someone you want something from, such as a bank loan, or a date! Do you think you would dress more carefully in one of those instances than you would if you were running to the grocery store, or meeting your family for a picnic?

Of course you would. And why is that? It is because you know that what you are wearing tells the world a great deal about you. Your outfit can scream "success!" Or your outfit can scream "I don't give a crap!" It matters, and deep down you know it matters a great deal.

In the same way that carefully choosing your outfit makes a difference, taking a few minutes to freshen up your pretty face can make you feel much more beautiful, more professional, and more successful.

Here's an interesting statistic for you. Did you know that when women are job seeking, 80% of employers would prefer hiring someone who wears makeup over someone who does not wear makeup. AND....to make matters even more unfair, women who wear makeup to work are 85% more likely to get promoted compared to those women who do not wear makeup.

Employers will always want someone who can pay attention to detail as well as represent their company in a professional manner. That's logical, right? If I'm choosing someone to represent me and my company, I want them to look good. Not like Mimi from the old Drew Carey show, but professional and pulled together.

Unfair, right? Oh well. *C'est la vie.* It doesn't matter if it's fair. The bottom line is, we need to look good for a myriad of reasons. The most important reason to look good is your own self-esteem.

Now that I have you understanding why it's important to wear a bit of makeup, I'm going to tell you that it's just as important that you not wear too much makeup either! If you look like you are going clubbing, or your face glitters like a disco ball, I'll advise you to back it down a notch. Although I will admit I love my glitter and sparkle, your look must always be appropriate to the situation.

If you are an all natural Ivory Girl and you need some help putting together a professional makeup look, head to your local department store and ask for a lesson. Likewise, if you have been wearing your disco ball makeup during the day, head on over to that same department store for a "tone it down" lesson - and make sure you buy something. Those ladies behind the cosmetics counters are NOT there for FREE.

Mindset Shift: **Accentuate** rather than **Spackle, Paint & Glow**

Once someone has shown you the proper way to apply your makeup for different occasions and reasons, you'll find that you are able to use that new skill to **accentuate** your beauty. This is a much better method than trying so hard to **spackle, paint & glow** your way into something you are not!

Ready for what's next my friend?...

Your Speech. Once again, different from your accent. Working on the way you sound might seem a little daunting to you. It was for me. I remember thinking *How in the world can I change how I sound without seeming like a crazy person!?* But it really wasn't that bad. I spent time recording myself on my iPhone and listening back in horror! Then I found someone who's voice I loved listening to. Luckily for me, she was a minor celebrity, so I could find a lot of recorded things to listen to. I would hear something she would say, and then I would say it back. I did this every day in my car. For me, that was the best place to find privacy for something that would sound ridiculous to anyone listening in. Of course, I still think I talk too fast and I still hear my accent, but I know that because I've made an effort to control my speech, it's better than it was. If this is something that you feel you struggle with, believe me when I tell you that you will never feel that it's perfect. You'll be practicing all of your life! Spend some time looking - or listening - for someone you like, because you will be listening for quite a while!

Mindset Shift: **Patience is a Virtue** rather than **Fake it till you Make it.** I don't think I need to add anything else here!

And now…

Your Heart's Desires. What do you love? Are you making a point of revisiting what it is you truly want and desire as compared to what you are expected to want? Interesting question? Don't know? That's ok. I am here to help you figure it all out. You may not know this, I know I didn't, but you get to choose your heart's desires. You aren't stuck with them. No one can force them on you. You do not have to accept what other people expect of you, either. That's the best part. Of course your parents always have something in mind for you as they raise you, but ultimately, once you're an adult it's your choice. How's that for good news??

Trust me when I tell you it will be worth every second that you spend determining what your real heart's desires are. Coming from a family that didn't travel anywhere other than the road trip to visit my grand parents each summer, one of my heart's desires has been to travel. Also, coming from a family that encouraged as much Plain Jane as possible, I also have a burning desire to find glamour, beauty and elegance.

Maybe your heart's desire is to visit a foreign country or to become a singer or dancer…or dentist, for that matter. Whatever your heart's desires are, it is time for you to choose them and then figure out how you're going to create them in your life. Knowing that you are in control of these makes it vital that you become aware of what they are. So just open up your mind and your heart. Ask yourself, in a perfect world where there are no limitations, financial or otherwise, what is it that you want to do? I know it's a big question, love. More answers are coming.

Mindset shift: **Embrace Your Dreams** rather than **Get Through Life**

Once you **Embrace your dreams**, you will welcome everything wonderful into your life, and you will build joy every single day. **Getting through life**, well, that's just not what God put us here for, now is it?

Are you ready for more?

Your Hair. "MY GOD! YOUR HAIR! YOU'RE WEARING IT LIKE THAT??" Thanks Mom.

WAIT JUST A MINUTE. LET'S TAKE A BREAK HERE.

Once again, the last thing I want you to think is that I'm suggesting we blame our parents for the way we live our lives. I seriously mean that. I don't blame my parents for anything that is happening in my life. Why? Because I am an adult. I am responsible for everything that happens to me. That's right. All of it. Yes, of course, my parents influenced my thinking, but guess what? They aren't doing it any more. I'm a grown ass woman and I get to choose every single thing and every single person that I allow into my life. *And so do you.*

Now...Back to your hair...

MY GOD! YOUR HAIR!! Trust me on this. The day you show up at your family's Thanksgiving dinner with hair that is different from the style you wore growing up, you will hear all the comments. Hopefully, they will be nice ones because you deserve it.

I know, I know. You smarty pants ladies are reading this and thinking, "Seriously? Hair? How silly! How frivolous!" BUT! If you are the lady who goes home and has to listen to everyone ask, "Who do you think you are? WE don't wear our hair like that. WE don't dress like that. WE didn't raise you like that. Who do you think you are?" Then you will LOVE a chapter that encourages you to choose your hairstyle the way you choose your education, your jewelry or your car.

Choosing a hairstyle is a very personal thing. When you have the perfect style, you feel like a ROCK STAR, right? But try out a new stylist because the person you usually go to has the measles and get a style that is not quite what you asked for, or worse, NOTHING like what you asked for, and watch out! Life turns poopy. Yes. Poopy.

Of course in my opinion, you are beautiful no matter what, but you don't need my opinion. Who's opinion do you need? YOURS.

And YOURS is the ONLY opinion that matters. So if you do end up with the bad haircut, I have three words of advice for you:

ROCK. IT. OUT.

Make it funky! Make it wild! Find a way to make it look as good as possible and OWN it. If you love it, others will love it. And if they don't, well so what??? You are going to ROCK IT! Until it grows out. And it will. I promise! That's how it works.

Mindset Shift: **Style it** rather than **Fight it. Fighting** it is a waste of your beautiful new energy. **Style it**, baby.

*****

Time for another break. Go get yourself a cup of coffee, tea, or maybe a glass of champagne! You deserve it!!! I, as always, choose Champagne! Pop! Fizz! Clink!

Do you see where I'm going with all of this yet? Life, love, looks and fabulocity are all about what? **YOUR** mindset. What are you thinking about? Are you loving and kind to yourself as you progress through life and make your journey towards finding out who you really are? Or are you mean to yourself ? Are you being gentle with yourself ? Are the things you tell yourself the things that you would tell your best friend?

One of my mentors calls it "The Girlfriend Test." When you are talking to yourself, if you'd say it to your best girlfriend, someone you love, someone you care about, then go for it. If not, throw it out and give yourself a new thought.

Let's keep rolling...

Your Weight. Ugh. One of the most difficult things that we talk about as women is our weight. This is a subject that we continually beat ourselves up about. Did we over eat? We hate ourselves. Did we choose the French Fries with Cheese rather than the Salad? We hate ourselves. Did you give in to that second bowl of ice cream while watching late night TV? We beat the sh*t out of ourselves. And on top of what we are doing to ourselves, we have to hear it from our friends and family. Believe me, if you lose weight and look great, someone will not like it! If you gain weight and look fabulous, someone will not like it! So what's a girl to do???

Read on...

I am aware that I'm not a doctor, and I don't pretend to be for even one second. But I am pretty freaking excited to tell you about this Mindset shift:

Don't get SKINNY. Get HEALTHY.

Skinny is ok. Looks good in clothes most of the time. **Healthy** = ROCKSTAR!!!

*****

When you get the not so nice comments from people in your life, please remember that the problem is not you. YOU are fabulous in every way. YOU are making growth decisions for yourself. YOU are creating your best life ever. Why aren't they?

The problem is this: When you make these types of changes in your life, the people who are closest to you will get scared. That's right. Scared as a bunny being chased by a dog. What are they afraid of ?

Here is where you need to channel your inner ANGEL, baby. Your GENTLE ANGEL. Your PATIENT, GENTLE ANGEL. And you need to remember these two very important facts:

1. People in your life ARE seeing you make good, positive changes and they are NOT making good, positive changes themselves. This shines a giant spotlight on them. Be kind to them. They are examining themselves through the beautiful, rose colored lens of YOU and wondering why they haven't been able to make these changes in their own lives.

2. They are afraid they are going to lose you. They are afraid that they won't recognize you any more. They are afraid that you are going to leave them. Again, I say be kind. These are not bad people. They are concerned that THEIR lives will be different because YOUR life will be better.

Bring out your heart. Just smile. Don't argue with them. Be a shining example of happiness and have the confidence of someone who is doing wonderful things in her life. You honestly deserve to be confident about what you are doing.

People have a tendency to get angry when they are afraid. If you are kind and patient with them, I bet you that second scoop of ice cream that some of these individuals will come to you privately to ask you what you're doing and how they can do it as well. Look forward to that day as you show kindness to those around you who just can't understand why you'd want to change anything about yourself.

And we're not done yet…

What you Read. One day my friend Cindy went to her home town to visit her mother. She arrived late in the evening and was pretty tired by the time she got to her mother's place from the airport. She told me that she was exhausted, and put her bags away and sat down on the sofa. Her mom was getting ready for bed, and Cindy was reading her book. "A Room of One's Own" by Virginia Wolff. Cindy told me that when her mom came into the living room and saw her reading, she walked over, lifted the book up so she could see the title, and just said, "Oh God, what the hell is THAT?" Without knowing it, her mother had seriously hurt her feelings. Her words sounded so judgmental and condescending that it made Cindy feel horribly embarrassed and inadequate. Great feeling, right?

Cindy said her mom might have been ok if she had been reading the Bible, but that it would have opened up a horrible conversation between them about how she was living her life - all wrong, of course. Cindy also might have been ok if she had been reading Twilight or Harry Potter. Because mom liked those books, they were good. Because mom had no interest in what Cindy was reading, it was completely ridiculous in her opinion. Which meant that Cindy was completely ridiculous. At least that's how Cindy saw it. And felt it.

What I have learned over the years and through all of the self reflection, mentoring and work I've done on myself is that I have a choice of how I react to another person's opinion. I have a choice of how seriously I take the opinions of anyone at all. Just because someone is not appreciating what I enjoy, doesn't mean I have to give them power over me or give them any credibility at all. I don't have to make their opinion more important than mine. I respect the opinions of others', but the bottom line is, it is my responsibility to accept my own situation and make the appropriate changes. It is your responsibility as well.

The way I react to someone else's opinion, is MY CHOICE! YOUR CHOICE. I really would like you to take a few minutes to think about that. We get to choose how - and if - we react. Of course, I want everyone to think I'm the most fabulous, smartest, prettiest, coolest individual ever - I'm a human female!!! But, I understand that my tastes are my tastes and everyone does not share them, and that is OK. Our choices make us who we are - make us individuals.

So what to do? Read whatever the hell you want. It's your choice and your business and no one, regardless of how close they are to you has the right to dictate how you choose to feed your mind.

Mindset shift: **I read whatever the hell I want to read. Period.**

One more and then I'll move on…

Your Beverage of Choice. Why is this an issue? Let me share. A good friend of mine grew up in a very strict, religious home where alcohol of any kind was strictly forbidden. She had a bit of a rebellious soul all of her life, so you can imagine how she might have fought the idea of no alcohol once she turned 21. She was respectful enough to not bring any alcohol into her home, but naturally thought nothing about having a glass of wine when she was out with her friends. She wasn't the type of individual to ever drink excessively. However, she did have to endure the pretty much constant berating and lecturing from her mother. Mom felt it was her obligation to be sure her daughter knew that her soul was in danger because of the 2 or 3 glasses of wine per week she enjoyed.

You can imagine her parents' dismay when she came home one day and announced that she was going to enroll in Sommelier School! Their beautiful, pure, perfect daughter! Now drinking for a living! And encouraging others' to do the same!

Well, after many years of denial and ignoring, she received a surprise. She went to visit her mother when Mom had just returned from a vacation. To my friends surprise, her mother had brought her a bottle of wine back from her vacation! It took a long time and many conversations, but my friend very respectfully held her ground and Mom realized that her relationship with her daughter was far more important than the constant fighting about whether or not alcohol was acceptable or sinful.

The moral of this story: Be respectful. Be kind. Stand your ground without imposing your views on anyone. My friend never brought alcohol to her mother's house. She enjoys a glass of wine with her friends or at her own place, away from her mother. She was happy and nice when she was with her mother, and both of them realized that their relationship is bigger than this issue. I have heard her say many times that her mother is her best friend. And this mutual respect came not from fighting and not from being disrespectful toward each other, but from loving each other and sharing.

Mindset shift: **Communicate** rather than **Demand. AND BE NICE!**

Now, please understand, I am aware that I've covered some topics that may seem frivolous to you, and may seem like things that matter very little at first glance. But remember that the DETAILS MATTER. Life, love, joy and happiness are all about the details in our lives.

Do something wonderful for yourself. Examine the details in your life one at a time. Take the time to give these details some thought and find some small, baby step-like changes that you can add or delete, and you'll find that life will change for you.

The way you think and the way you react to the people who love you, will be the magic ingredient that shifts your life into the direction that you choose.

NOTES:

The Good, the Bad and the Family

Let's just get this thought out there and out of the way: The people who are closest to you in your life, will most likely be the ones who support you the least. It was that way for me, too. Why is that? Because, as I've already said, your growth shines a giant spotlight on the lack of growth in others.

That doesn't mean that you shouldn't better yourself or make the changes that you desire to make in order to create a beautiful life for yourself. It just means that you have to take into consideration the reaction and push back you may receive from those individuals who are in your life.

Also, the last thing you want to do is automatically eliminate the people who have been a part of your life until now. The best thing you can do is include them in your changes to the degree that they will allow you to do so.

Everyone has to deal with the various people in their lives, whether they are family or friends or those who raised them. In relating to and dealing with the people around you, there are a few things that I would like you to be aware of. Hopefully, some of these ideas will help things go smoothly for you as you make the transitions you choose to make.

First, everyone has that person in their family who I like to call the "contrary." This is the individual who never agrees with anyone. Ever. On anything. This person can argue during a Monopoly game or a religious exchange equally. This person is never ok with anything that anyone is doing. They always have an opinion and can always provide 3 or 4 reasons why whatever is happening will never work. Can you identify this person in your life? Be prepared with clear thoughts and words when you are around this individual because they are masters at undermining others.

If you're the first person in your family who has ever gone to college, this person will let you know that you are wasting your time. If you're the first person who spends time on their appearance, this person will tell you that you're being too vain and self-centered. You have two choices with this individual. Either prepare your answers for their negative comments, or don't let them know what you're doing. Everything I share with my mother...ahem...will be on a need to know basis. Yes, my contrary is my mother.

Another person you will run into will be the individual who tells you that you are fabulous and wonderful and they are oh, so proud of you, but then they will run to everyone else in your family and tell them that you are out of your mind. Awwe, sweetie! You don't think you have someone like this in your family? Well you do. You'll recognize them eventually. In the meantime, be prepared for the occasional phone call from someone who you haven't spoken to in ages, asking you if you are all right and if you need help or someone to talk to.

Then there's the brother. At least there's my brother. Judgmental and holier than thou. He knows best, and it is in your best interest to let him feel like he is correct about that. Possibly even Dad. They love you unconditionally - as long as you're staying exactly the way they knew you when you were young. It's all good. Just let them love you. Do they really NEED to know everything you're doing? Probably not!

The most important thing for you to remember is that the changes you are making are YOUR changes. No one has to accept them. You are the one who is changing things up, so you are the one who will have to make the allowances for the people you love in order for them to be around you. That doesn't mean you should accept any abuse or excessive negativity, but you do have to be understanding and know that it will take time for people to understand that you are actually improving yourself. Your self-improvement has nothing to do with your family or friends' opinions, attitudes, or beliefs, but they may make it about themselves from time to time. Be strong, my heroine!

You are making an effort to better yourself and change your attitude, style, appearance, likes and dislikes. You also need to make an effort to introduce all of this gently to the people who love you, in order to avoid alienating them. I am not suggesting that   you   must baby people, but again, understand that what you are doing is all new and foreign to them. That being said, remember that there is NOTHING wrong with you. You do not need to be fixed or repaired or anything of the sort. If the people in your life try to make you feel like there is something wrong with you, always remember this:

It's not you, it's them. No, it's you. It's definitely you. And you should be damn proud of yourself !!!

Pop! Fizz! Clink!

Eventually they'll learn to understand and accept you. And now it's time to get ready to make more beautiful choices and changes. Let's get to it!

TIME TO CREATE!

It's time to look more deeply into all of these vague changes I've been talking about and get into the glam and glory of actually getting it done.

So where do we start when we're thinking we'd like to improve our lifestyle and our attitude and our way of being? It's not as difficult as you may think, although you will need to make a few tough decisions along they way. But don't worry! Nothing is set in glitter glue around here. As you grow and progress through your journey, you may find yourself making changes by adding and deleting past decisions! That's the Brilliance of this entire exercise! It is all about YOU, my darling. YOU and no one else. Are you ready to start calling the shots in your own life? It's about damn time, don't you think?

First of all, let me ask you a few questions. And if I were you, I'd get a journal to make notes - I hear there is a FABULOUS one available on Amazon! And it just so happens to be written by *MOI*! (*shameless plug!*)

It's time to start dreaming! I want you to put yourself into a place of BRILLIANT PERFECTION! No limitations, no financial issues, no family stress, no job stress, just perfection. It may take a few minutes for you to get into this state, but it is very important. Have you ever played the game, "What would I do if I won the lottery?" It's very much like that. Allow me to set the stage for you:

No limitations. No financial issues. No family stress. No job stress. Can you *imagine????* Someday is NOW. The world is your runway! Your oyster! Imagine having all of the time and money you need right now. Feels like a weight off of your shoulders, right? No family stress? I think we've been there and done that! No stress of any kind!

Take a few minutes and place yourself there. I'll wait.......

Still waiting.....
Still waiting.....

Now that you are *feeling* this way, it's time to start making some notes. I've left room for you to write right here in this book. (use a pencil, in case you change your mind!) ***Get excited! Here we go!!!***

STEP ONE:

1. What do you love? What do you love about yourself ? What do you love about your family? What do you love about your home? Your husband or partner? Your style? Your clothing? Remember, write out ONLY what you LOVE, not what you want or hate!

_____
_____
_____
_____
_____
_____
_____
_____
_____
_____

2. What makes you laugh? What makes you feel all giddy inside? What gets you excited and pumped up? Tickled inside? Children? Puppies? Roller Coasters? New make up? New shoes? A clean house? A Chanel bag?

_____
_____
_____
_____
_____
_____
_____
_____

3. In a perfect world, what would you do for a living? What would your dream job look like? Would you be some kind of performer? Would you choose to work alone on a book? In an office? Would you work with children? Animals? What type of job would make you *jump* out of bed in the morning?

_____

_____

_____

_____

4. In a perfect world, how would your house look? Imagine that it is decorated perfectly! You don't need to change a thing! Describe it in detail, as if you already have it exactly the way you want it!

_____

_____

_____

_____

_____

_____

_____

5. In a perfect world, how would you dress every day? Write as if you already have the wardrobe of your dreams! As if you know exactly what you want your style to look like! Do you have a go-to style that almost feels like a uniform (in a good way!) Describe your beautiful wardrobe as if you already have it all put together!

_____

_____

_____

_____

_____

_____

6. In your perfect world, what do you do to take care of yourself ? Do you eat well, do you exercise? No more of those orange Dorito fingers for you! No more guacamole under your nails! Are your nails perfectly done? How often do you go for your Mani/Pedi? No more horse hoof heels for you! Do you love to read? What do your morning and night time skin care routines look like? Remember, this is a PERFECT WORLD!!! What do you do to take care of yourself PERFECTLY!!

_____

_____

_____

_____

_____

_____

_____

_____

_____

_____

I hope you found this exercise fun and that you've made lots and lots of notes. Remember that this is just a start and we'll get into more detail, but for now, let me share something with you. I have learned that when I'm analyzing my life and deciding where I want to make changes and create joy and brilliance, the more grateful I am for what I already have, the more I receive.

Now, I don't want to go all woowoo on you here, but once again, remember that everything you do and everything you have is energy. Whether you believe that it all comes from God or you believe that you manifest it all yourself, it is energy. And the more good energy you put out into the Universe, the more good energy you will pull back into your world.

I'm all for good energy, with or without understanding why it works. Aren't you?

STEP TWO:

Now we're going to go through all of the notes you've made, one at a time and slowly. Think about how you were feeling while you were making all of your "perfect world" notes. Did you feel excited about the possibilities? NOTE: If you didn't feel excited about what you were writing, then go back and do that exercise again. The purpose of this is to create the *feeling* of those possibilities. Imagine that every single thing you wrote is available to you *right here, right now!*

Look at your answers to question one. How would you feel if you had exactly what you wrote down *RIGHT THIS MINUTE?*

Write that feeling down here:_____

Look at your answers to the second question. How would you feel if you had exactly what you wrote down *RIGHT THIS MINUTE?*

Write that feeling down here:_____

Do the same thing for each of the questions I asked you during Step One.

Feeling from question Three:_____

Feeling from question Four:_____

Feeling from question Five:_____

Feeling from question Six:_____

Take just a minute and think about those six feelings? Now that you think about it, are those feelings true and accurate? If not, go back and do the exercises again. It is just fine if there is some duplication. You don't need to be creative with your words. Remember this is not about being fancy. This is about *you and your own feelings.* You are beginning your journey. This exercise may take you some time. Do not rush. Do the exercises over and over until you feel that you've generated the appropriate and excited feelings for each question.

STEP THREE:

Write all of the feelings in a straight line here: *Humor me!*

_____

_____

Now take a look at your list of feelings. There should be some pretty exciting words written down. The most exciting part of all of this is that those feelings make up exactly WHO YOU ARE. I want you to read these words and I'm going to ask you to think of them as your *style.*

What exactly is your style? The words you've written down that describe how you feel will enable you to clearly define your style. And these *style words* are really what we're going for. These are the words that describe who you are. And yes, I am aware that I had you complete this lesson in the mindset of the perfect world, but guess what? *YOUR PERFECT WORLD IS RIGHT NOW.*

You are going to use these words to describe exactly who you are right this minute. I suggest that you keep them with you every day and use them to create the exact life you want to live.

Here is your new responsibility to yourself: As you go through each day, with every decision you make, you must ask yourself, "Does this decision lead me closer to the life I want, or move me farther away?" This is how you will set yourself up for success in creating your beautiful new lifestyle!

Remember that everything is energy and by doing everything you can do to live in this *Style* right now, you will attract and create the beautiful life you want to live. RIGHT. NOW.

I want to share my personal Style Words with you. Once I chose my Style Words, and began to keep these words in mind as I went through every day, I found that decisions, choices, attitudes, and everything I wanted opened up for me. I was drawing what I wanted toward me by putting that specific energy out into the Universe. I know you will attract what you want as well.

Here are my style words: Confident, Elegant, Worldly. And that's just me. This is my style. You need to get clear on yours. Then with every decision or choice you make, as you use your Style words as your guide, you will lead yourself towards your most Brilliant Life!

Learning that you are in complete control of designing your life can be a very exciting revelation! And it's even more exciting to know that this is going to happen for you *right now*!

STEP FOUR:

Are you ready to take some positive, energetic, on purpose action? Think of one thing you can do right now, today, that would help you to embody your new found Style! This will become something you will want to do every day. Add one thing to your to do list that will lead you toward your new style. *NEW STYLE = NEW YOU!!!*

Straighten something in your house, clean out your handbag, clean out your refrigerator, throw away some junk food, schedule a mani/pedi. Anything you would like. Just take some action. What did I do? I de-cluttered my closet, and then donated everything that didn't bring me joy or suit my style.

Once I did that, I felt like a new woman. So now it is your turn. Go feel like a new woman!!! You'll find it very freeing and empowering.

Gosh, this is my favorite chapter! You are discovering real, tangible things you can do right now to feel your best and begin to create your most Brilliant Life EVER!!!!

Now would be an excellent time to do a bit of brainstorming with yourself! Make a list of things that you would like to do, see, add to or delete from your life. Don't worry about the timeframe or when you think you'll be able to fit these in. Just make your wish list and you can come back and revisit the list later!

I keep a perpetual wish list going! ALWAYS, when an idea comes to me I make note of it and just add it onto my list. I review my list once each week or so and look for things that I can fit into my schedule. Now, THAT is powerful.

I am going to give you lots of room for notes on this page. Just add, add, and add some more! It will be your *secret*! And there is nothing wrong with a woman having a few secrets, right? It's good to keep the mystery alive and keep people guessing!

READY? GO!!!

_____

_____

_____

_____

_____

_____

_____

_____

_____

_____

_____

_____

_____

_____

_____

_____

_____

_____

_____

_____

_____

_____

_____

_____

_____

_____

Consistency & Flexibility

Once we are able to get clear on the feelings we want to hold onto as we move forward making the changes and improvements in our lives, then we have to ask ourselves, now what? What do I need to do with those words? With my life? Aside from keeping them on my mind everyday, what do I do next?

The first thing you need to do is go easy on yourself. As you move through your day and ask yourself if you are approaching brilliance or walking away from it, you need to be kind to yourself. Some of the changes you will make will be more difficult than others. Of course that doesn't mean you stop or give up. When you reach a difficult place, you have to move gently and tenderly with yourself. Slow down, sit quietly for a minute and ask yourself why it feels difficult. Are you moving too fast? Did you not allow yourself enough time? Are you sure this is something you want to do? If the answer to that question is yes, then ask yourself this: HOW CAN THIS BE EASY? Thanks to Tonya Leigh and the French Kiss Life, this is my favorite question. If you ask yourself this question, you will get an answer, I promise!

Remember that what we're doing here isn't a one day, one weekend project. This is a journey and it is an ongoing seeking out of what and where and who you want to be, and what changes need to take place in order to get you there.

Honestly, some days it's going to look like you barely brushed your teeth! It might look like you need to start all over again. And when that happens, I want you to know that everything is just fine! You are in great company and there are many, many other people out there who are on the same type of journey that you are on.

I recommend that you pay attention to how you feel when you speak your style words out loud. Keeping them in your head is fine, but you need to say them out loud and *feel* them all over again. I do this every single day, and every single day I get excited about my chosen style all over again.

If at some point you feel that some of the excitement may be wearing off with one or more of your words, then just repeat the lesson in Chapter 5. If you'll remember, I said right in the beginning that you will be making changes as you go through this process. Especially if you've never done anything like this before. So again I say, go easy on yourself.

That's where the need for flexibility comes into play. You know what you need to do, you've made decisions about what types of changes you'd like to see in your world and you're taking steps to get there. When you hit a bump in the road, examine it, accept it, decide if it is truly the right direction for you, and keep moving forward.

I promise you that once you've completed Chapter 5 a few times, you will get very clear on your style words and you will then gain a clear understanding of who you want to become and how you'll go about becoming that person.

Let's talk about consistency for a moment. As you continue your journey, you'll find that sometimes those bumps in the road feel more like brick walls. Ouch! That is completely natural and normal. You have been doing things a certain way for a very long time, right? You have to expect that the old you is going to resurface from time to time and you will need to put her in her place - gently. And with love.

The sweet little you, who you still love and understand, only wants to keep things comfortable. Don't get angry with her. Give her a hug and ask her how she's feeling. You may find that she feels like she no longer knows who she is and she is very confused. But remember this, my love. You have her back. These changes are going to create joy and brilliance in your life and hers, so don't freak out about becoming a bit uncomfortable.

As a matter of fact, keep this in mind. When you are uncomfortable, this is when you are about to learn something about your self. There is something to be excited in that whole idea, isn't there? When you start to notice that sense of not knowing how you're supposed to feel, or why you feel the way you do, *celebrate!!!* Something wonderful is about to happen! Pop! Fizz! Clink!

When we begin to see those scary, insecure feelings as something to celebrate, it makes the experience a lot more enjoyable. I've gotten to the point where I get really excited when I start to feel a little uneasy! The last time I felt that way, I learned that I wanted to create a self-study program for my clients. When I poured myself into that, I started learning more and more about myself and how I wanted to show up and contribute to the world.

All good news, right? So to those uncomfortable moments in life, I say: BRING IT ON, BABY!!!

What do you have to celebrate today?

Out With the Old & In With the You

By now you see that "WHO DO YOU THINK YOU ARE?" is all about DECIDING who you want to become and getting all your ducks in a row, so you can become that person. So it's time once again to take action and make some strategic moves.

Let's find an area that you would like to change in your life, based upon your style words, and get you going in that direction. Sound good? I will show you how the process works, by using one of my style words as an example.

I believe that the word, *Elegance,* and the idea of creating a more elegant life, is something that many people can relate to. In our world of hurrying and rushing and trying to get a hundred things done each day, I know there are many people who want to calm down, feel a bit more in control of their lives, and live more elegantly. If elegance is not your thing, that's ok. Just read through the process, because this applies to any change you're wanting to make.

ELEGANCE - The Process

Here's the big question: How does one go about editing, creating, adding, deleting, building, and then living elegantly? Do you think you can become elegant one day, suddenly? Why YES you can, mon cherie! It did however, take a bit longer than one day for me, I will admit to you.

I remember feeling impatient once I had made my decision, and I had to stop and remind myself: This is a journey and our definitions of elegance may change from time to time, which means the actions we take will change. What was elegant to me when I first started my journey is not what I would consider elegant right now.

Elegance is a relative concept. If you are used to shopping at discount stores as I was, then choosing to try out your shopping experience at your local Department Store should feel like you are incorporating elegance. However, if you shop only at Saks Fifth Avenue, choosing higher-end styles will be your route to up-leveling your elegance factor!

Let's look at the bigger picture. The first thing I did, once I chose *elegance* as a style word, is take a look at the physical condition of my surroundings. Did I live in an elegant environment? Two words: HELL! NO! I never had! I had to take the time to figure out how I could begin to live in elegance in my home, and that took some serious thought and work. All fun, don't get me wrong, but serious.

I chose to start in the one area of my home where I spend the most time. I knew that it wouldn't be completely elegant any time soon, but I made a list of what I needed to do in my family room and my kitchen. It made sense to me to create elegance where I hang out the most. I felt I could create some instant gratification!

But when I looked around my family room and thought, "Holy Clutter!!" I felt completely overwhelmed! Where do I start? I saw magazines, some not even read. A vase of dead flowers. Pens and pencils and Sharpies all over the place and coffee cup rings on the coffee tables. Yes, I dust and straighten, but I was always able to look past those coffee, water, soda rings. No judging, please! I was busy - that's my story and I'm sticking to it!

My family room is pretty large, probably 24' by 24'. Working within that room, I chose to divide it into 5 sections and I started to give it some thought, one section at a time. Breaking it down, baby!

I had a small wine rack/desk combination that worked well as a place to keep my computer and writing items. That was a keeper. Except that I had papers and pens and printer ink and forms and my cell phone, and scissors and 2 old coffee cups, a pencil sharpener, a photo of my dog, 3 candles and a hair band cluttering up the tiny work area that I'd chosen for myself. Sounds like I'm kidding, but I'm not.

This was an easy fix. I found a really pretty box that I could keep on the desk to hold all of my items together and out of site. Tres chic! Then, I found the most beautiful coffee cup I could find. It happened to be a gift from my step-daughter Bonnie, and it has a French theme to it. In that cup went all of my pencils, pens and scissors. Do you see where I'm going with this? I need most of those items on my desk, but not laying around cluttering things up!

I decluttered the hell out of that little desk and I was so proud of myself! I kept one or two pretty items out, which I saw as elegant, and I hid everything else! Also, since it doubles as a wine rack, I got out some Chateau Montelena wine and put it in the wine rack. I'll have to dust off those bottles occasionally, but it looks very elegant and purposeful! One small area has been transformed into a tiny piece of elegance in my world! Pop! Fizz! Clink!

Next, I changed out the old yellow and green crochet blanket that I had thrown over the back of my couch with a beautiful cream colored cashmere throw that I found on sale! Elegant!

I cleaned everything out of the fireplace, since Winter was over and we were "enjoying" 103 degree weather here in Dallas, and I replaced those old ashes with flameless candles. I even found some with a remote control feature! Chic chic chic!!!

I moved all of the furniture, one piece at a time so I could vacuum under everything. You know as well as I do that THAT chore doesn't get done very often, and I wanted to start fresh!! The things I found under there! Scary!

Once I saw the momentum building, I really went nuts! I was so excited about how things were coming along, that I cleaned everything off of the end tables, and left them with only a lamp. I stacked three beautiful coffee table books like a pyramid on the main coffee table and placed a small vase of flowers on top. I put away all of the movies that were left out. I removed the clutter of random unmatched candles from the mantel of the fireplace and replaced them with just a few that matched so that it looked less cluttered and more intentional.

This was an easy project, actually. With each item that I picked up, I asked myself if I loved it, or if it just showed up one day to fill space. If I couldn't think of another place within my house where it would be a beautiful, elegant addition, out it went!

Now, when I enter my family room, I see a comfortable, clean, elegant room, where I'd be proud to have someone drop in on me unexpectedly. Also, I made a point of keeping everything simple.

This way it is easy to keep clean. And every time I clean, I feel a wonderful sense of appreciation and gratitude for each elegant item that I own.

The next weekend, I went into my kitchen. Everything in the kitchen is clean, because I have always felt motivated to keep it clean. The bad news there is that it was cluttered beyond belief! How does one go about creating an elegant kitchen? That took some effort. But in the end I asked the same question I asked in the family room. Do I love it? Did it just show up one day to take up space? Do I use it?

I went through everything, down to my plastic containers and made sure they had lids, and threw away anything that didn't have a partner. That freed up space in my kitchen cupboard for all of the appliances that I used occasionally, but chose to keep out because I loved them back when I purchased them - years ago! I cleaned my counters well, shined up the stainless steel appliances, got rid of the random items, papers, etc. that found their way into the kitchen, and it actually felt elegant to me!

I'm certainly no Julia Child, but my kitchen does matter to me, so once I felt good about the way it looked, I also felt better about preparing meals. Rather than eating a snack out of a bag, I was excited about getting out my pretty serving dishes and making each meal feel special and elegant. That included background music and candles during dinner - even when I dine alone!

I ended up taking the kitchen project one step further and I went through all of my coffee mugs - you know, the ones that I brought back from that quick South Beach trip. The one that had my old company logo on it. Yuk! Get rid of THAT!!! And I decided that as part of my elegant journey and as a way of approaching my desired style, I needed to drink my morning coffee out of a beautiful coffee mug. I found a gorgeous one at Neiman's. Freakishly expensive, and not even crystal, but I only needed one, so I went for it! *Voila! Tres chic cafe pour moi!*

Does that sound silly to you? Am I going into too much detail? I thought so at first, but do you remember a few chapters back when I said, "the details matter?" Well they do. Every single detail matters.

Every beautiful detail moves you forward to your beautiful life. Add as many beautiful details to your life as you possibly can. When you surround yourself with these beautiful little details, you create the life you want to live. In my case, it was living elegantly.

I am still working on this and probably always will be, because it is my journey and I enjoy the process. I promise you that once you get started, you will enjoy the process, and especially the results!

To reinforce what this chapter is all about, I'm going to give you a few more ideas of some beautiful details that you can easily - and inexpensively - add into your life to create a special environment that creates the feeling of the life you want to live.

Declutter. Look at every area within a room, one space at a time and see what you can eliminate, rearrange, or clean up.

Fresh Flowers. Flowers are Nature's Chanel. Add them into your world and you will love the feel they create in a room. You can get them at the grocery store. They don't have to be expensive, just pretty. And PLEASE make sure you replace them when they die!

Background Music. This adds a wonderful ambiance to any room. When you are choosing yours, make sure you love it! If you love Top 40 Radio and it inspires you to feel elegant, then go for it. Maybe you love the feel of classical music. Jazz. Reggae. Remember, you don't need to know everything about the type of music you choose. You just need to choose music that creates the feel and mood you are looking for. I happen to love movie soundtracks. I've been known to play the soundtrack from Midnight in Paris over and over because I love that movie so much. I also love the soundtrack from Oblivion when I feel that I need some alone time. It makes me feel isolated, but in a good way.

I also change out my music seasonally. I love Trans Siberian Orchestra and Mannheim Steamroller at the Holidays! Ask yourself what MOVES you musically? And then add it to your home. In the family room, in the kitchen, in the bathroom. Pandora is your friend!

A few other ideas for adding some of the important little details:

A crystal tumbler on your bedside table. A red solo cup does not scream elegance! Make it go away!

Beautiful, luxurious soaps in your guest bathroom. But much more importantly, beautiful, luxurious soaps for YOU in YOUR bathroom.

A gorgeous, decadent scented candle in your kitchen, bedroom, and several in your bathroom.

A champagne flute by your bathroom sink to use when you brush your teeth. Why not? Instant glamour!

Beautiful serving pieces for your dinners. And now that TJMaxx HomeGoods has entered our lives, none of these things have to be overly expensive. Just look around you. Where can you add a detail or two that will add elegance, beauty and glamour to your life?

*****

I want to thank you for indulging me as I have shared with you a few of my ideas for creating the details I've chosen to add into my world. It feels really good to talk about these things and I know you'll feel better and better about your life with every little detail that you allow into your world.

*****

Once I finished the first project, it felt easy to move all around my house and my life and declutter everywhere I could. I decluttered the junk in my car glove compartment, to my closet, to my jewelry box, to my junk drawer in the kitchen, to the top drawer of my nightstand, to my make up and my sock drawer. I know that once you get started, it will be just as easy for you to keep going as it was for me.

Also, once you begin this decluttering process, you'll feel a great sense of freedom. Freedom from miscellaneous items that you no longer need, freedom from items that were just taking up space and weighing you down, and freedom from the past, as little by little, you bring more elegance and your own style into your world!

I have one more thing I want to touch on before I end this subject, and it is in regards to discovering your personal style. I'm talking about your clothing, shoes and accessories, what you accumulate in this area and how you want to present yourself each day.

One of the best things I ever did in my life, was take the time to discover my personal style and then edit and declutter my clothing and accessories, so that my wardrobe was a direct reflection of my chosen style.

I'm not just talking about downsizing your clothing or donating your old shoes and gloves. This is about making a conscious, intentional decision about who you want to become. How do you want others to see you? How do you want to see yourself and what image to you want to project?

As I mentioned, I've always been a Francophile. I love the way European women choose to dress. I love their simplicity and elegance. I love how they can look different every day with a relatively small selection in their wardrobes. I have adopted this style and simplicity as my own, and let me tell you once I did that, dressing every day became a fun and fast adventure!

I choose to have only black and neutral staples in my wardrobe. I do still have a few pieces of color, but very few. All of the color I add to my outfits comes from the accessories I choose for the day. Whether it's a colorful handbag, a sparkly clutch or a brilliant Hermes scarf, or colorful shoes, this is where I choose to express myself.

It makes buying clothes so quick and easy. If I find a pair of pants that fit perfectly, I will usually buy 2 pair. And always in black. This just works for me. Here is my personal motto: BLACK, GREY, NUDE, REPEAT.... That's just me.

You may love color. You may love dresses. You may hate black basics, and that is great news! This is all about determining YOUR personal choice of style.

I know that when I walk into a room, 90% of the time someone is going to complement me on my outfit. You need to choose a style that represents who you are and get comfortable with the complements. They are on their way. Once you determine your style and embrace your choice of clothing on a daily basis, it will begin to mirror your personality. People will notice that it makes you happy to dress in your personal style. Get ready for people to ask you how you do it, too!

"How do you always look so pulled together?" Is my new favorite question!!

Simplicity is elegance! And dressing in YOUR personal style is elegance, and sophistication. Remember that you are in charge of deciding who you want to become. You are responsible for making the choices and becoming that individual.

If you have been paying attention and making some moves, maybe even some notes in the margins of this book, then my love, you are well on your way!!

"How do you always look so fresh, pretty and elegant?"

NOTES:

New You, New Habits

As you may guess, all of the changes we're making in our lives are going to take some time, some practice and some commitment. As I keep saying, this is a journey, and there will be times when creating the NEW YOU feels like the hardest work you have ever done.

I am going to ask one thing of you. Now that you've made it this far in your journey - **please trust me.** I've been through it. I've been where you are. I did not start out with all of this "FABULOCITY" in my life. I started at a big ZERO, and you may feel that way as well. By trusting me, you will see that all of these small changes will result in a life filled with elegance, happiness and joy. So….Trust me my love. I will not lead you astray!

Now, for some more good stuff….

They say it takes 21 days to form a new habit - or break an old one. I will challenge that and ask you to allow yourself 90 days. Slow down and savor life!

You can change your body in 90 days. You can change your home in 90 days. You can change your relationship in 90 days. Anything you focus on consistently for 90 days will change for you. In fact, any-thing you focus on consistently for 90 days will roll over like a puppy for you!

And here is a little more insight for you that I learned from one of my mentors years ago. The inspiring, beautiful and talented Pamela Waldrop Shaw, National Sales Director for Mary Kay Cosmetics taught me this:

"You can do anything in 90 days. 90 days is magical. During the first 30 days you feel like you've worked like a dog and see nothing. Ever feel like that? So you have to keep going. During the second 30 days, you feel it coming. You don't actually see it yet, but you feel it coming. During the third set of 30 days, you start to see the results of your consistent and persistent efforts."

This is why it's important to keep going and learning and growing. Once you start to see small changes and some consistent shifts in your mindset and your actions and your attitudes, an entirely new form of excitement will come into play for you.

It's like dieting. Once you start to see the results from your efforts, the excitement and momentum will enable you to keep going.

And speaking of dieting, would you like to know how I embraced the 90 day cycle, and lost 25 pounds in three months without dieting at all? Well, here is a "habit" that I strongly recommend you create. This is all about your food choices.

The food we enjoy is truly a gift from the Universe. If you think about it, everything we enjoy from fancy dinners to popcorn in front of the TV is a gift to us. It nourishes us - most of it - and it keeps us alive. Therefore, we must treat it as a gift.

Here is my *"Thank you Universe for everything you've given us"* diet plan. You can eat anything you want. Anything. But eat it with gratitude and eat it in appropriate amounts. Small amounts. Conservative amounts. Remember that you will get to eat again in a few hours. You don't need to eat everything in your house in one sitting.

Another one of my mentors, Tonya Leigh from French Kiss Life says, *"Eat until you are elegantly satisfied."* I love this. Only Tonya could come up with something that beautiful.

Ask yourself this: How much would you eat, if you were standing at a beautiful buffet at the Ritz Carlton Place Vendome in Paris, wearing a gorgeous designer, floor length gown, in the company of Royalty, sipping Veuve Clicquot?

Would you eat small amounts, gracefully, aware of your surroundings and aware of who you will be speaking with next? Well, THAT, my friend is how I lost 25 pounds in 3 months. I ate absolutely anything I wanted. In small quantities. And I chose to eat only the most exquisite food I could find. I ate only the highest quality chocolate. Only fruits and vegetables that were in season. The leanest meat and the only the best, crusty bread I could find. I dipped the bread into truffle oil, rather than slathering it with butter, and it was exquisite. And I didn't eat the whole loaf of bread. I asked myself if certain foods were worth the calories. A Snickers bar? No, thank you. A beautiful chocolate mint truffle from Godiva, absolutely. But just one. Per day.

Now don't get me wrong, I have had more than my share of orange Dorito Fingers. I've scrubbed the orange mystery-cheese-powder off of my hands from the bowl of cheese popcorn that I love. And I am sure it will happen again from time to time. But not daily. Not weekly. Every now and then. I want to keep that weight off! I choose to eat only the best in moderate portions because it FEELS ELEGANT to me. I find there is no need to panic about it. There will always be more food later! ***Thank you, Universe!***

Let's talk about some of your new habits and that 90 Day Plan. I choose to use a datebook/journal to keep track of my 90 Days. That way I have a clear starting and stopping point with what I want to accomplish. I'll sit quietly and choose what I'd like to focus on for the next 90 days. What habit do I want to embrace? What habit would I like to break? How do I want to see myself 90 days from now?

Perhaps, now you've decluttered parts of your home and you want to keep it that way. You might want to begin the habit of every morning or evening walking through your newly decluttered home and straightening things back into the way you want them. We all know that things move and change during the day based upon what we are working on, so it will take some maintenance to keep things decluttered and feeling elegant. Choosing a time of day to regroup your mind and your home, and making a point of doing it consistently for 90 days will create that habit for you. After the 90 days is over, you will just automatically do your walk through every day or night. You won't need to schedule it. You will have created a beautiful, elegant habit.

How about your bed time routine? Do you go to bed with your makeup on? Coco Chanel would roll over in her grave if she knew! So create a beautiful ritual for your bedtime and make a commitment to maintaining that ritual. Find luxurious skin care and high quality bath towels and make a ritual out of washing your face each night.

Light a candle that makes you feel beautiful. Allow yourself that one special (small) piece of chocolate while you're getting ready for bed. If you have a family or significant other around, close the bathroom door so you have the privacy you need to complete your ritual every night. Make a point of continuing this practice for 90 days and again, you will find that you've created the most luxurious experience for yourself! You deserve this! You deserve to take luxurious care of yourself, so make that part of your 90 day plan!

How about creating the wonderful habit of making dinner special? Even if it is left overs -fabulous ones, of course, and even if it's just you! Why not use beautiful dishes? What are you saving them for? The after-life?

Light a candle or two on your table. Put on some beautiful music! Set pretty place settings and use the cloth napkins. Make each meal special. There is no reason you can't use pretty dishes for breakfast, lunch and dinner. As my step-mother always says, "The dishwasher doesn't care how many dishes are in there." Can you make this part of your 90 day plan? If you do, you'll have another elegant habit under your Gucci belt!

If you are like me, there will be about 1000 things you'd like to make part of your 90 day plan. But I suggest that you choose just a few at a time. Remember, the 90 day cycle starts again every 90 days! You will be looking at what you've done and what you've accomplished at the end of each cycle. It is at that point that you can let some of the ideas go because now they are a part of your elegant, daily life. As time goes on, you will add one or two more things that you want to build into who you are becoming. I find this process very exciting. The beauty of the gradual progression toward becoming the best YOU that you have ever seen, is such a joy to watch.

Here are a few things that I incorporated into my life by using this 90 day plan. I am certainly not suggesting that you copy my life - and even if you wanted to, it changes so frequently - like yours will - that you won't be able to do it. These are just a few things to get you thinking creatively.

In prior chapters, we discussed dealing with the push back from family and friends who cannot understand that you are trying to better - to up-level - your life. Now that you are learning how to deal with that aspect of your life, let's get moving and make those changes permanent!

Here are some possible NEW HABITS for you to incorporate into your beautiful new life! I'm leaving some space between each one for notes.

Get yourself a pretty pen! Ready?

1.De Clutter the following areas:

1. Clothing

2. Shoes

3. Handbags

4. Accessories

5. Home

6. Car

7. Bedroom Closet

8. Drawers of clothing

9. Books

10. Jewelry

11. Kitchen Gadgets

12. Kitchen Counters

13. Bathroom Counters

14. Linen Closet

15. Makeup & Hair Care

2. Add Candles to your daily life!

3. Create Evening Rituals, Skin Care, Music, Candles etc.

4. Create Morning Rituals, Skin Care, Music, Candles.

5. Create a journaling practice that works for you.

6. Find a Fragrance you love and wear it every day. Wear it to bed.

7. Choose beautiful lingerie - or nothing at all - to sleep in!

8. Find something in your life to celebrate every single day!

9. Make conscious decisions about what you will and will not allow into your life and stand by your new rules.

10. Be generous with your time and resources. Give back. Volunteer. Share your talents.

Remember, this list is just to help you begin to think about what you can do to add elegance, glamour, excitement and happiness into your life. This list along with YOUR list will help you to create the feeling you want to have every single day of your life.

What else can you add into your life RIGHT NOW, that will help you to create the life you want to live? You do not need to be perfectly lined up with the sun, moon and stars to begin living a beautiful, brilliant life. In fact, any given day, you'll most likely find something that doesn't look or feel perfect to you. We're not looking for perfection. We are looking for brilliance and happiness.

Approach making changes in your life with the mindset that life isn't perfect, so every move you make isn't going to be perfect. Do everything you can do to enjoy the journey. Appreciate the fact that you are making the journey enjoyable. Creating joy and happiness are most important. Remember to find the humor!

As you are aware by now, all of the changes that you're going to want to make are beautiful, but some days, the cat will eat your flowers and your boss will make you work through your well planned lunch hour.

Just breathe and make the best of it. Remember that the down times show us the contrast we need in order to appreciate the up times!

Are you starting to think about the new habits you want to add into your life? I gave you a long list and you will have plenty of your own to add to that list, I am sure.

Please remember that you cannot do all of them in one 90 day cycle. Just choose one or two or three that make you FEEL GREAT! Start with those first and watch the magic happen. Get ready. Your life is about to become BRILLIANT!!!

One Day at a Time

Rome wasn't built in a day my love, and neither was Paris, Venice, London, Newark or Pittsburgh. And I don't want to break your heart, but you too will need more than a day to evolve.

We've shared a great deal of information throughout this book and a lot of great ideas. But Super Woman or not, you cannot implement everything at once. So take that burden off of your shoulders right now and relax. In this chapter, I'm going to help you pack your bags for your journey toward Brilliance.

Let's talk priorities, babe. You already know that you can accomplish anything that you want if you are willing to focus on it for 90 days. Good. Got that. So what should we focus on first?

Well, let me ask you this: What do you want? To find that answer, let's go back to that perfect world we created in the beginning. In your perfect world, where there are no boundaries, money is no issue, time is no issue, and you can have whatever you want whenever you want it....What would you choose as your first step?

Wow! BIG question. And there's that bigger question we discussed before: How do you want to FEEL? Do you want to feel free? Powerful? Abundant? Elegant? Sophisticated? Worldly? Loving? Thin? Smart? Slim? Chic? Savvy? Give yourself a few minutes to think about this topic again because that is exactly where we are going to start.

Reminder: Living a beautiful and brilliant life is not about having THINGS. It's about creating the FEELING of what you want. A special Thank You to beautiful Tonya Leigh of French Kiss Life for introducing me to this concept!

Example No. 1 If you want to feel thin - and who doesn't? - then find things you can do in your life to create that feeling of being thin right now. If you were to incorporate these things: eating well, exercising, eating more slowly, dressing in clothing that makes you feel thin, you would feel thin right now. BEFORE you actually lose the weight.

Actually getting thin will take some time, and that is ok. Remember our approach, anything you want to eat is fine, and when enjoyed in small portions, you will get where you want to be. No excessive food denial, just logic.

Eat less, weigh less. This, in combination with doing what you can to feel thin right now, will enable you to begin to live the beautiful life you want right now.

Example No. 2 If you want to feel worldly and you haven't done much traveling, how can you feel worldly right this minute? Well, you could plan a trip. Or you could begin reading about the places you'd like to visit. Although, actually visiting a place is the way to go, until you are able to do that, why not learn about those places? The more you learn about various places in the world, the more you will be able to speak intelligently about them, and the more you will feel worldly right now. BEFORE you actually get to go. And bonus! Having great conversations about the world is stimulating and fun, and you will be Oh! So sophisticated and worldly!

Example No. 3 If you want to feel cultured. Go get some culture! There are Libraries and Theatre Companies and Symphony Orchestras and Choral Groups all over the world! Go to a museum! Have you ever been to one? No? Then go in, buy your ticket and tell the person at the information desk that you've never been. I promise that person will be nice to you and tell you exactly where to start.

Find your city's cultural directory online. Just about every city has a website with various events listed that are happening locally, exhibits that are coming, etc. Find something that interests you and GO! If you don't have someone to go with, make a date with yourself and go. You will be surprised at how quickly you'll learn what type of art you love, what kind of theatre or music you love. The more you make a practice of doing these types of things, the more cultured you'll feel. And I would bet big money that you'll make new friends as well as find current friends who share those same interests that you didn't know about!

Example No. 4 If you want to feel elegant in your home…pretty much all the chapters leading up to this one covered this. It's your home! Make it elegant. Clean it. Re-arrange it. Spruce it up. Scent it! Light it up with candles. You can create that elegant feeling right now. Start with one room and then move on! This is all in your hands and under your control!

Once you know how you want to feel, making decisions and setting priorities will become much easier for you. For every feeling you have or want to have, there are steps you can take to create, build on, and push yourself toward exactly how you want to feel. Now THAT is elegance!

*****

Again, I ask you to TRUST ME. And GET MOVING!!!

The only thing that will hold you back from generating the feelings and the life that you want to have is you. So get out of your own way, and take some action!

Make yourself feel beautiful and powerful first thing in the morning by setting your intention for the day. You can do this by journaling every morning. It should only take you about 15 minutes each morning to write out something that you are grateful for and then remind yourself of the choices you've made and how you want to feel for the day. Take at least one action every day that will feed into creating the way you want to feel.

And go easy on yourself. I am aware that I am talking about making all of these changes in your life as though you just have to snap your fingers and they'll be done. You and I both know that's not how it works. It takes time and energy and consistent action to make real and lasting changes in your life. So be kind to yourself.

Understand that this is YOUR journey. Not mine, and not anyone else's. You need to take it at your own pace, without giving yourself permission to do nothing. And that being said, there will be days when you'll do nothing. While I was writing this book - exactly at this spot - I had done absolutely nothing for 2 solid days. I had contracted an icky, summer time cold and felt like death warmed up! I did nothing but rest, sleep, watch a movie or two and drink orange juice. (Super fattening, by the way, but I allowed it because I was ill.)

There are going to be days when you'll just need to retreat into your cave and take care of yourself. And I am all for that! Do you have a "cave" that you can retreat into? Maybe it's your bedroom, your bathroom, or den. It really doesn't matter where it is, as long as you have the privacy you need to be still and be calm.

Do you have what you need in that space so that you can nurture yourself and get back to feeling great again? For most of us, our cave is our bedroom. That is where my cave is because I've made sure it is as welcoming and comforting as possible. If you don't have a cave, then I suggest you make it one of your first priorities. You will love having a place where you can slow down and be alone from time to time.

My cave is ever-evolving, but there are things in there that I know will always make me feel comforted and nurtured. Inside my cave is a stack of inspiring books that I am reading one by one. Each book has something that I want to learn or be part of or bring into my life. I have a few movies that I can go to when I want to be swept away. I have beautiful and sensual candles. I have my signature, custom made perfume - and yes, I wear it to bed every night. I have crisp white sheets on my bed and crisp white Frette Pajamas that always make me feel elegant. They were pretty expensive, but I chose to make that expense a priority because the feeling I get from those pajamas is priceless, and I will have them forever. I have a Mason Pearson hairbrush. It makes me feel special and pampered. I have a Baccarat crystal water goblet on my bedside table because I allow only the exquisite into my life. For me, these are the items that make me feel pampered, special, comforted when I'm down. I suggest that you begin to surround yourself with whatever it is that makes you feel that way, too.

Why take time for this? Because you are worth it, my dear. You deserve it, my darling. You have earned it, my love. And you alone are responsible for creating your world of happiness. So go now, and build yourself a cave!

*****

There is freedom in knowing that this can be a slow journey. This is nothing that you need to rush toward. You must take your time, choose who you want to be, choose how you want to live, choose with whom and with what you want to surround yourself. Then you will have the freedom to take the steps to make it all happen. First, by creating the feelings you want and then allowing the life you desire to find you.

It is up to you to set the priorities. What is most important to you? Add that into your 90 day cycle. Then what, then what, then what and THEN what? Just keep adding what you LOVE into your 90 day cycle and you'll begin to see the magic happen.

I am SO excited for you! I've been practicing all of this for quite some time and I'm farther away from where I started and closer to the life I want to live than I ever thought possible. Just know that if you are implementing what you're reading in this book and thinking about the woman you desire to become, you are well on your way to living your most brilliant life!

The Whole Package

So now that we've spent such a great amount of time discussing the fact that you have always had the power to define and realize who you are, you must accept who you are, be thankful for the way you were raised, choose who you want to become, and create that life without guilt, you're golden, right?

Yeah. Me too. Again, I want to remind you that this is an ongoing process and not a definite destination. That is actually a really good thing! Let me tell you why!

As adult women, we sometimes hesitate in making decisions because we feel that once we make a decision, it is a commitment we have to keep for the rest of our lives. As though every decision were a marriage or something! I know, I know. Bad joke. But seriously, I admit, there are some decisions in life that are permanent! Ask me about the poor choice of tattoo I have on my body.

However, keep in mind that the decisions you are making about your life right now, using the ideas and processes I've laid out for you, are not cast in concrete! Nothing is written in waterproof mascara! All of the decisions that you make in determining how you want to live your life and who you want to become, can - and will - change as you grow. The wiser you become, the more skillful you'll become at making your life decisions, and then one of two things will happen. Either you will not have to change the decisions that you've made, or you'll be just fine with changing them on a regular basis.

For example, I once made the decision to de-clutter my life and live more simply. I know that I will never want to change that. I know myself well enough to know that simplicity is what I love and I always will. However, I have also decided that in order to create my cave, I only want white linens, pajamas, towels, slippers, white white white, and I love the feel of that. Perhaps in a few years, I'll run into something pink that makes me feel AMAZING!!! Then, I may want to change out all that white cave stuff for pink cave stuff.

I may decide that I want to be Vegan and that will knock my idea of what the perfect meal looks like for a loop! I may decide that I only want to wear red high heels and have to make changes to the all neutrals in my wardrobe that I am so happy and excited about at the moment. I may decide that I'm going to hire a cleaning lady and be forced to rely on her skills to keep my house clean.

The point is, we cannot forget that *The Whole Package* is actually a moving target. As we grow and as we learn, we will make changes to who we are and how we want our lives to look.

Right now, I love Ballet. My daily work out is Ballet inspired. I'm loving Degas Ballerina paintings and sculptures. I love light piano music in the background because it reminds me of the Ballet. My next love might be Hip Hop (doubt it, but you never know!) Then out goes the Ballet and in comes Kanye West.

Because I - and now you - have learned that you are in charge of who you are, what you do, and the type of life that you choose to live, there are always going to be changes. As we grow, our tastes and likes naturally become more refined and we will make those changes accordingly.

Now that you are seeing your life, the whole package, as a moving target, I would like you to view it as an exciting opening up of your world! The more you allow into your new life - on YOUR terms - and the more you learn, the more life will open up for you.

By putting yourself out there, you are aligning yourself with the Universe so that more goodness can come to you. When you think about it that way, there is no limit to what you can do or who you can become. On page 1 of this book, you may have decided to do a certain thing or handle a situation a certain way, but by page 88, you know that you have the power to decide anything and make any decision you want. You also know now that the world is your Runway and you can change it up at any time! So keep an open mind. Allow things in that you may have never considered possible before and you will grow like you've never seen yourself grow before!!!

I think now is a good time to for you make a few more notes.

1. Write down a few things that you've decided you want to make happen in your life. Be as vague or as detailed as you'd like. You can write things like, make some new friends, remove some "frenemies," declutter something specific, learn something specific, learn a language, visit a new place. Anything that has come to mind while reading this book, write it down.

2. Set your 90 day plan so you can accomplish some of the things you've chosen. Choose to create some new habits as well as some beautiful new facets to your life. You are a sparkling diamond and it's your time to shine!

3. After the first 90 days, come back here and look at your notes. It will be a beautiful learning experience for you to look back and see what you had originally chosen and how those things worked out. Also, and even more empowering is learning where one specific choice you've made has lead you down a road to other choices.

This is where the magic happens. The more intentional action you allow yourself to take toward what you truly desire in your life, the more happiness and joy you will find coming back to meet you half way.

NOTES:

Your New Responsibility

So here we are, approaching the end of this book. Now that you have gone through the information, hopefully have learned a few things about yourself and your life. You have moved up a rung or two on the invisible ladder of this beautiful life we have been given, and you need to be aware of some new responsibilities that are given to you.

Don't freak out - they are all GOOD responsibilities!!!

1. You understand that all people change and why change is sometimes necessary, painful or not. Your responsibility: **Accept change, no matter how it feels at the moment.**

2. You have learned the most important question you'll ever ask yourself. *"Who do I want to become?"* Your responsibility: **Ask it. Always ask it. Ask it all the time!**

3. You are now aware that you are capable of choosing the mindset that you need to have in order to be your best possible, Brilliant self. Your responsibility: **Choose the appropriate mindset always, and you'll choose to feel powerful.**

4. You have learned that when people lash out, or give you grief about the person you want to be and the way you are choosing to live your life, they are doing so because they care and they are afraid of losing you. Your responsibility: **Be gentle. Don't hold this against them. Stand your ground lovingly.**

5. You have learned that if you stop running around in circles and take a quiet moment to think about what you love, what you want and who you want to become, you can create an action plan to get yourself there. Your responsibility: **Do the work.**

6. You now know that there will be bumps in the road as you grow. This isn't all sunshine, rainbows and unicorn poop. This is where you learn about yourself and apply consistency and intention. Your responsibility: **Bandage those knees, get back up, and keep going.**

7. Once you decide who you want to become and what you want in your life, it's time for implementation. Now you get to look around your life and make the changes that you feel are necessary in order to support who you are becoming. Your responsibility: **Make it happen, and make it happen NOW. Take ACTION.**

8. You have learned that in order to become the woman you desire to be, you must create some new habits. You've learned all about the 90 day cycle and how to make it happen. Your responsibility: **Get into that 90 day cycle routine with your habits and desires.**

9. You have learned that you can create the feeling of what you want long before you actually have what you want. Your responsibility: **Start creating the feeling of what you want into your life right away in order to attract what you truly want.**

10. You have learned that there is no completion date. This brilliant lifestyle is an ongoing reaching out and pulling into your life of what you really want. The wiser you get, the more you'll change. Your responsibility: **Roll with those changes, baby! You've got the power!**

11. To illustrate the most important responsibility of all, I will share a quote from the Netflix Series, House of Cards. Frank Underwood, corrupt but very successful says, **"If you're lucky enough to do well, it's your responsibility to send the elevator back down."** So, if this has been helpful to you, share the information with someone else who would benefit from it. **Send the elevator back down.**

One Final Note

When reading this book, my own book, I've thought a few times, why do all of this? It sure sounds like a hell of a lot of work. Wouldn't it be easier to just sit on the sofa and have Orange Dorito fingers? Well, I think it would be easier in the beginning. But look ahead 5, 10, 15 years into your future. I believe I would have many regrets if I lived to be 90 or 95 years old and didn't have good stories to tell. I would regret never having learned French. I would regret not having learned to sing opera. I would regret not having made the wonderful friends that I have made. I would regret not having the stimulating conversations with the exquisite people I now surround myself with.

And looking back at my past, I have made more than my share of mistakes and had my share of missed opportunities. It wasn't until I was in my 40s that I took a good, hard look at my life and made the decision to change how I was choosing to live. I decided to embrace my past and do what I could to learn from it. The moment I made that decision, the world became bigger and more accessible to me. My dreams turned into possibilities. My feelings were suddenly all good. Even the sad ones. They were and are, all under my control.

It wasn't until I discovered my mentors, Cara Alwill Leyba, Founder of The Champagne Diet, and Tonya Leigh Rising, Founder of French Kiss Life, that I realized I have the power to choose and allow only the exquisite into my life. *Suelement L'exquis.* Both Cara and Tonya have shown me that we all deserve the exquisite and there is nothing wrong with carefully choosing - curating - what I do and do not allow into my life. In addition to all of the items I've mentioned in this book, this includes people.

I have several people in my life who represent the exquisite. Cara, Tonya, Connie, Jacquey and others. Some are new friends and some are old friends. One in particular has been pulling on my heart strings for many years, and he had absolutely no idea that he was doing so. It wasn't until I found myself leaving a place permanently, and contemplating the thought that I may never see him again, that I felt I had to take some action. I needed to move past my fear and have a serious conversation with this man, and I could not move forward without making that happen.

I was uncharacteristically nervous and shy, and so afraid of sharing how I felt and the possibility of having him laugh at me. But the thought of never seeing him again and keeping this secret that I had inside of me forever was far more painful than the vulnerability I was feeling about sharing what was in my heart. I truly felt compelled to step up and have the talk. If I hadn't been able to overcome my fears in the area of a potential loving friendship with a wonderful person, what credibility did I have in continuing to write my books and in advising others?

Well, I did step up. And let me tell you, he seemed very surprised at what I had to share. Guess I'm a pretty good actress, because he had no idea that I found him to be one of the most intriguing, intelligent, thoughtful, beautiful people I had ever met. I am happy to share with you that my thoughts and ideas about this man were absolutely on point. When I spoke with him, he handled my shy, blushing confession about how I felt, with dignity, grace and respect. He asked questions like, "Why me?" without vanity, and he asked me to explain all of this to him so he clearly understood where I was coming from. I hope he wondered why I had kept it all to myself for so long. I honestly don't know why I was so shy with him for all of those years. I guess being the girl I am, a constant work in progress, made me feel vulnerable to someone for whom I had the utmost respect and admiration.

I hope and pray that he will always be part of my life and always be my friend. He's been supportive and available to me when I needed someone to speak with about my career, my books and various choices I've made. I truly love and appreciate him.

Why am I sharing this with you? It is because I want to encourage you to step up, share your heart, speak out. If you are intrigued by, in awe of, or even in love with someone, let them know. We are all human, and I believe that when someone is loved, in the end, it is always better for them to have known.

That's the biggest piece of beauty in this whole lifestyle concept! When you embrace this lifestyle, there will be no more stagnation and no more intimidation in your life. You have the power to build the life God gave you into exactly what you desire.

Life is for those pay attention, take control and share.

*****

We are the creators of our lives, the nurturers of our souls, the tellers of our stories, the interpreters of our pasts, our decisions, and our dreams…

…and for this, we must thank the Universe.

NOTES:

NOTES:

NOTES:

NOTES:

NOTES:

NOTES:

A SPECIAL THANK YOU

As I write my books, it seems that I have started the tradition of adding a special Thank You to some very important people. There are always so many people involved in my life and in my work and it seems this has become a great place to say thank you. As in the past, many of the people listed here will have no idea that I have listed them, and if someone shows them, they may not understand why. This is a perfect example of how we never know who we are going to influence, and who will never forget us, for the rest of our lives, regardless of how limited or extensive our contact has been.

So once again, and in no particular order:

Cara Alwill-Leyba, Tonya Leigh Rising,
Hank Coennen, Victoria Elder, Rob Escher, Deb Garber
Martine Campbell Marechal, Shana Paladino-Ripp,
Kenny Lucero, Julia Zaman, Marcus Wyss,
Mimi Cervera, Gita Adib, Mary Kay Ash, Denise Brown,
Chrissy Manasia, Carl Sagan, Lisa Robertson, Christiaana Rote,
Coco Chanel, Michelle Lambrou, Don Bodine, Linda Hamblin,
Geraldyne Van Arnam, Tammy Elliott, Brenda McCoy,
Lisa Mallard, Jacquey Avery, Maureen Saladino, Eddie Coennen,
Kristen Small, Anastasia Dunn, Liz Seacrest, Dan Achtermeier,
Wafa Alhafi, Aimee Culler-Ross, Brandi Earl,
Libby Easton-May, Connie Mikolic, Bonnie Gipson,
Bobbi Mayhew, Gigi Grossman, Allison Hunter, Vicki Hutto,
Christopher Gleason, Seth Burnes, Julie Martin, Tina Osvalt,
Jennifer Spencer, Kay Thompson, Brandon Ferrante,
Robert Ferrante….and so many more.
Thank you for everything you have taught me. Whether you understand why or not, you are in my heart.
Love,
Donna